BestMasters

Mit **„BestMasters“** zeichnet Springer die besten Masterarbeiten aus, die an renommierten Hochschulen in Deutschland, Österreich und der Schweiz entstanden sind. Die mit Höchstnote ausgezeichneten Arbeiten wurden durch Gutachter zur Veröffentlichung empfohlen und behandeln aktuelle Themen aus unterschiedlichen Fachgebieten der Naturwissenschaften, Psychologie, Sozialwissenschaften, Technik und Wirtschaftswissenschaften. Die Reihe wendet sich an Praktiker und Wissenschaftler gleichermaßen und soll insbesondere auch Nachwuchswissenschaftlern Orientierung geben.

Springer awards **“BestMasters”** to the best master’s theses which have been completed at renowned Universities in Germany, Austria, and Switzerland. The studies received highest marks and were recommended for publication by supervisors. They address current issues from various fields of research in natural sciences, psychology, social sciences, technology, and economics. The series addresses practitioners as well as scientists and, in particular, offers guidance for early stage researchers.

Paula Friedrich

To be healed or to be hacked

Ethical issues and concerns about the use of VR and AI in mental health care

Springer Vieweg

Paula Friedrich
Julius-Maximilians-Universität
Würzburg
Würzburg, Germany

ISSN 2625-3577 ISSN 2625-3615 (electronic)
BestMasters
ISBN 978-3-658-50066-5 ISBN 978-3-658-50067-2 (eBook)
https://doi.org/10.1007/978-3-658-50067-2

This Springer Vieweg imprint is published by the registered company Springer Fachmedien Wiesbaden GmbH, part of Springer Nature.
The registered company address is: Abraham-Lincoln-Str. 46, 65189 Wiesbaden, Germany

Foreword

If you or someone you know has thoughts of suicide or struggles with their mental health, you can reach out to the following resources for support: 'Telefonseelsorge' - call 0800 111 0 111 or 0800 111 0 222, 24/7, 'Nummer gegen Kummer' - for children and adolescents: call 116 111. You are never alone.

Competing Interests The author has no competing interests to declare that are relevant to the content of this manuscript.

Abstract

The prevalence of mental health disorders amounts to more than 970 million affected individuals worldwide. The limited number of mental health care professionals is unable to cover the demand of care, resulting in long waiting lists and an increase in sick days taken due to mental health issues. To relieve personnel and provide accessible tools, the use of AI and VR for the treatment of mental health disorders has been researched for many decades. However, research exploring the deployment of embodied AI within a VR setting remains scarce. Therefore, this study first assesses mental health patients' biggest concerns about the use of AI and VR for therapy in an online questionnaire. The answers to the open questions and ratings of most important factors revealed the importance of Data Autonomy and Transparency about the embodied AI in line with prevailing ethical principles. In the main study the effect of Transparency and Autonomy on self-disclosure and trust towards the embodied AI was explored in an in-person VR study. Results suggest a higher level of self-disclosure when higher Data Autonomy was provided. This effect, however, did not translate for higher sensitive questions, mirroring lower levels of disclosure found in therapist-patient interactions when discussing more sensitive topics. Transparency did not influence level of self-disclosure and both Autonomy and Transparency showed no effect on trust towards the AI. Additionally, an effect of gender on trust was found, showing higher levels of trust for women compared to men. This work contributes to the ethical discussion around AI in mental health care with a human-centered AI perspective and insights into patients' concerns on this development. Moreover, it explores a first approach to transforming ethical principles into tangible technical implications.

Contents

List of Figures

List of Tables

1 Introduction

30 seconds of silence. In November 2024 the meditation app Calm uses their ad space in popular American TV channels during the presidential campaign to grant viewers thirty seconds of uninterrupted peace and hereby aims to raise awareness about mental health. Every one in eight people suffers from mental health issues, amounting to around 970 million affected people worldwide with numbers only increasing, particularly with the outbreak of the Covid-19 pandemic (World Health Organization, 2022). The amount of people in need of treatment, however, are difficult to cover with the limited numbers of available mental health care professionals, resulting in long waiting periods and in turn a failure to provide timely care (BPtK, 2022).

Artificial Intelligence (AI) has become an integral part of our everyday lives and manifested in various parts of society. Either through chatbots on a website, remote- controlled vacuum cleaner or smart speakers—AI has revolutionized today's technology and the way we communicate. The advancements of these new technologies have also been recognized for the usage in mental health care to, for example, efficiently analyse large amounts of data (D'Alfonso, 2020). This not only facilitates the diagnosis of mental health disorders but the treatment thereof through e.g., text- or speech-based interaction with patients. Combining the use of AI with *Virtual Reality* (VR) or using VR as a stand-alone approach, the generation of virtual worlds can help display stimuli, for instance, in the context of treating anxiety disorders, like fear of flying through exposure (see Rothbaum et al., 2006). The benefits thereof and its deployment have been emphasized and encouraged by the German Ethic's Council and the Council of Experts to mitigate the shortage of skilled workers in healthcare (Ethikrat, 2023; Sachverständigenrat, 2024). Using these technologies can help affected individuals by increasing the accessibility of care and allow an overall relief of mental health care professionals.

P. Friedrich, *To be healed or to be hacked*, BestMasters,
https://doi.org/10.1007/978-3-658-50067-2_1

However, the risks of AI are manifold. AI appears to have the possibility of causing great harm through issues like spreading misinformation and reinforcing bias of training datasets (see Kordzadeh & Ghasemaghaei, 2021). In 2016 Microsoft, for example, introduced their AI chatbot 'Tay' and let it interact with users on the social media platform X, at the time known as Twitter. After 24 hours the chatbot had to be taken down as it expressed racist and sexist comments and demonstrated hurtful behavior, which it had learned through reviewing content on Twitter (Wolf et al., 2017). This incident reflects important aspects that need to be considered when designing AI and hereby utilizing *Machine Learning* (ML), the process of training computer models to mimic the way humans learn and act autonomously (IBM, 2025). Another example of this is a discontinued recruiting tool from Amazon, which showed a negative bias against women as they were not seen as eligible to hire for managerial roles (Dastin, 2022). Moreover, in 2024 news broke, reporting the AI chatbot Character.AI designed for role play to supposedly be responsible for a 14- year-old boy committing suicide (Montgomery, 2024). It shows the power AI can hold and reflects the worries prevalent among the population. Specifically, in a field such as mental health care it is crucial to acknowledge the sensibility of the information shared and the importance to design and implement safe and controllable technologies. Therefore, many ethical guidelines have been formulated, which address relevant implications to design ethically supported applications (see Fiske et al., 2019). The topic of data safety and the disclosure of sensitive data does not just entail signed consent but might in fact appear to users as though they are 'giving a piece of them away' (Margulis, 2011). Consequently, it affects users' overall interaction with technology and whether they feel safe to disclose their personal information. The field of *Human-Computer-Interaction* (HCI) continues to emphasize the importance of user-centered design, i.e., designing *for* the user. Similarly, the concept of human-centered AI has gained importance over the years (Auernhammer, 2020). Whilst there are prevalent ethical guidelines addressing the risks of AI in mental health care, it is yet to determine whether patients suffering from mental disorders are comfortable in disclosing their issues when interacting with AI and which factors affect the acceptance thereof for mental health care. The collection of data allows higher personalization, a more accurate training of AI systems and the linkage of different health care professionals to provide an encompassing treatment approach. But how can people's data be collected and protected simultaneously?

How are technologies designed that cover both ethical guidelines and make their users feel secure when disclosing their personal data? To collect aspects that might hold people back from using AI for the treatment of mental illnesses, the pre-study of this thesis aims to answer the following explorative research question:

RQ1: What are the concerns regarding VR and AI in mental health care, specifically regarding data security and how can they be accommodated within further development?

Through assessing participants' biggest concerns and the most important factors for AI and VR usage in mental health care, further research questions were proposed:

RQ2: How does transparency regarding AI and data collection affect self-disclosure and trust towards the embodied AI?

RQ3: How does autonomy regarding AI and data collection affect self-disclosure and trust towards the embodied AI?

This work aims at identifying concerns of mental health patients within an online study to move towards human-centered AI. Further, the effects of provided autonomy and transparency are explored in an in-person VR study utilizing an embodied AI. Ultimately, these efforts contribute to the ethical discussion around AI in mental health care and the comparison of legally required choices and information specified by the General Data Protection Regulation (GDPR) and the AI Act, with increased control and information.

The following thesis first provides a general theoretical foundation, most relevant for the topic of this work. Furthermore, the measures of the pre-study and its results are discussed. Additionally, the implementation of the project and the embodied AI is described, followed by measures of the main study with the respective results. Finally, all results are discussed and approaches for future work are suggested.

Theoretical Background 2

The following theoretical background describes relevant literature about mental health disorders and the treatment thereof as well as the use of Artificial Intelligence (AI) in mental health care, research focusing on the treatment of mental disorders using Virtual Reality (VR), virtual agents and lastly prevalent ethical guidelines and data safety laws regulating these new technologies.

2.1 Mental Health Disorders and Treatment Approaches

Mental health care has gained popularity in recent years with many celebrities openly discussing their own mental health issues, and organizations like the World Federation for Mental Health (2024) declaring the 10th of October as the World Mental Health Day to raise awareness about unseen struggles individuals might be going through every day. Similarly, literature also shows an increase in Mental Health Literacy (Furnham & Swami, 2018). To understand the broad term of mental health, it might help to first look at the definition of mental disorders. The World Health Organization (WHO, 2005) describes *mental disorders,* oftentimes also referred to as 'mental illness' as a 'significant disturbance in an individual's cognition, emotional regulation, or behaviour' (p. 1). It is often characterized by strongly affecting the patient's ability to function in society and aggravating normal everyday activities (Njoku, 2022). Mental disorders can happen regardless of gender, cultural background or age with research also showing a considerable number of children and adolescents affected by mental illness (Polanczyk et al., 2015). The prevailing stigma around mental illness manifests in negative attitudes towards people with mental disorders, which aggravates their standing in society and affects the disclosure of mental health issues out of fear of judgment (Hsiao

P. Friedrich, *To be healed or to be hacked*, BestMasters,
https://doi.org/10.1007/978-3-658-50067-2_2

et al., 2015; Read et al., 2006). But can mental health thus be defined as the sole lack of disturbance in emotional regulation?

Fusar-Poli et al. (2020) argue that mental health is not solely constrained by the absence of mental disorder, but entails many different aspects of social, environmental or economic nature. The World Health Organization (2005) has stated that there is 'no health without mental health' (p. 11), which encompasses the wide-reaching consequences of decreasing mental health and the interdependence of mental and physical health (Bhugra et al., 2013). Mental health can therein affect someone's physical health, with research showing, for instance, consistent stress to be very damaging to physical health and increase the risks of chronic illnesses especially for older or unhealthy individuals (McEwen, 2008; Schneiderman et al., 2005). This does not only, however, concern affected individuals but manifests on an institutional level, as an increase of sick days taken due to mental health issues has been noted in the past thirty years, resulting in less available workforce and ultimately affects the economy negatively (DAK, 2024). *Mental health* is ultimately defined as an ability to navigate stressors of normal everyday life, the ability to maintain one's role in society, such as forming affectionate relationships, and acknowledge one's own skills and value (Bhugra et al., 2013; WHO, 2005).

In 2019, 970 million people worldwide were suffering from mental health disorders (World Health Organization, 2022). Research shows a variety of different mental disorders, the most prevalent being *anxiety disorders,* which the National Alliance on Mental Illness (NAMI) estimated to be at a total of around 19.1% for adults in the USA (NAMI, 2023). The American Psychiatric Association (APA) describes *anxiety disorders* as 'disorders that share features of excessive fear and anxiety and related behavioral disturbances' (APA, 2013, p. 189). While fear is understood as the response to a real threat within the immediate future, *anxiety* is described as the anticipation of a future threat and is often accompanied by avoidant behaviour. Various disorders fall under this umbrella term, e.g., *agoraphobia, selective mutism, social anxiety disorder* and *panic disorder.* The *generalized anxiety disorder*, for instance, describes a general feeling of anxiety regarding various events, whereas *specific phobias* are characterized by the 'anxiety about a specific object or situation' (APA, 2013, p. 197) and consist of five different types, i.e., situational, animal, natural environment, blood-injection-injury or other. The situational type includes, for example, fear of flying or driving. The natural environment type entails phobias like a fear of heights or darkness. Thus, for fear of heights (acrophobia) a high building would be labelled as the *phobic stimulus.*

These specific phobias might follow a particular traumatic event that the individual experienced themselves or has observed other people go through. Apart from anxiety disorders, *depressive disorders* take up another large number of mental disorders in society. They are mostly characterized by 'the presence of sad, empty, or irritable mood, accompanied by somatic and cognitive changes that significantly affect the individual's capacity to function' (APA, 2013, p. 155). This entails the inability for individuals struggling with a mental disorder to participate in everyday life, strongly decreasing their quality of life. Anxiety disorders often lead patients to avoid situations which elicit fear, therefore, it might result in the avoidance of regular parts of life, such as taking the stairs instead of the elevator or even being around people and ultimately interfere with living a fulfilled and joyous life. Moreover, mental disorders, specifically depression, are highly correlated with suicide, resulting in an average of more than 720.000 people ending their life every year (WHO, 2024).

A common treatment approach for both depression and anxiety disorders are medication and *psychotherapy*, i.e., the practice of talking to a mental health professional about one's issues. The two approaches can be followed independently or simultaneously, depending on the type of disorder. A literature review suggests that patients suffering from depression disorders tend to prefer psychotherapy over medication and often oppose prescribed antidepressants due to a fear of becoming too dependent on the medication (Van Schaik et al., 2004). Moreover, anxiety disorders, specific phobias in particular, oftentimes remain untreated as individuals might feel as though their anxiety is 'normal' or does not warrant a psychotherapeutic treatment (Bandelow et al., 2017). Within psychotherapy, the approach of *cognitive-behavioral therapy* (CBT) is primarily deployed for the treatment of anxiety disorders. Kaczkurkin and Foa (2015) discuss the two most common types of CBT, namely cognitive therapy and exposure therapy. Whereas *cognitive therapy* mainly focuses on the re-programming of the patient's cognitive and behavioral patterns, *exposure therapy* is characterized by confronting the patient with the phobic stimulus and changing the information stored in the fear memory, and thus slowly decreasing the anxiety connected to the stimulus. The exposure to the feared stimulus can happen through imaginal and in-vivo exposure. Specifically, the latter has shown to be the most effective for specific phobias as it consists of a direct, not just imagined, exposure with the phobic stimulus (Kaczkurkin & Foa, 2015). Imaginal exposure also proves difficult as various mental disorders elicit high avoidance of thoughts or feelings of the feared stimulus or event. Whilst various studies have shown the effectiveness of in-vivo exposure therapy (Foa et al., 1985; Michelson & Mavissakalian, 1985), it can be difficult to confront the patient with the phobic stimulus in real life, as it might be hard to reach within a therapy session and is often not covered by patients' insurance. Therefore, the deployment of VR can establish easily accessible and realistic environments.

2.2 Virtual Reality in Mental Health Care

What is VR and how do the experiences of an artificial environment allow the alteration of thoughts or minimizing fear in the real world? VR can be defined in a variety of ways and is mainly characterized as an immersive, simulated environment, which a user can interact with through a *Head-Mounted Display* (HDM) that projects the environment on a portable screen. Various factors play into creating a convincing virtual environment, such as congruent sensorimotor experiences, like audio feedback, objects moving accordingly, and thus eliciting a feeling of presence in VR, i.e., the sense of being somewhere (Kardong-Edgren et al., 2019; Strickland, 2007). Slater (2009) has defined the VR-relevant concepts of *Place Illusion* (PI), i.e., level of presence and *Plausibility Illusion* (Psi), i.e., the credibility of a scenario. A third concept has been introduced regarding the ownership of one's virtual body in VR (Slater et al., 2022). Therefore, it is important to create the right level of congruencies and minimize breaks in illusion, allowing the same effects for e.g., exposure therapy in VR as in real life.

Particularly for the treatment of specific phobias, *Extended Reality* (XR) can be deployed easily. Juan et al. (2004), for instance, attempted to treat a patient's fear of cockroaches by exposing them to cockroaches within an *Augmented Reality* (AR) setting, i.e., virtual cockroaches were inserted in the real environment seen through a HMD. Within their study, the user was able to kill the cockroach and alter its size, and change the number of displayed animals. The experiment was conducted with one individual diagnosed with specific phobia of the animal type and during the exposure a therapist was present, guiding the participants throughout the session. Results showed that the simulated cockroaches were able to elicit anxiety within the participants. After the VR exposure the participants killed a living cockroach, underlining the success of the therapy session. Further work showed the ability of an AR exposure intervention to maintain its effects one month after the exposure (Botella et al., 2005). Moreover, Garcia-Palacios et al. (2002) developed a *Virtual Reality Exposure Therapy* (VRET) application for the treatment of spider phobia and were able to acquire similarly effective results. The participants were all diagnosed with specific phobia for spiders and the 23 participants were randomly assigned to the two groups, VRET and no treatment. While there was no set number for the duration of the treatment, the research group determined a criterion for the treatment to be completed, namely if a patient was able to hold a virtual spider while experiencing low anxiety levels. This included tactile feedback, i.e., the patient's hand touching a toy spider. Anxiety levels significantly decreased for participants of the VRET group. Additionally, the level of avoidance was measured using the *Behavioral Avoidance Test* (BAT), which showed a significant decrease in avoidance levels after the treatment compared to the condition undergoing no level of treatment. Whereas patients only interacted with a virtual spider during the VRET, the values for the BAT in interaction with a real spider decreased simultaneously. Garcia-Palacios et al. (2002) detected no dropouts, which highlights the attractiveness of a VRET. VR and AR exposure therapy appear to be as effective for the treatment of small animal phobia as in-vivo exposure therapy. However, Suso-Ribera et al. (2019) argue that in-vivo exposure therapy might be preferably considered when anxiety levels in patients are relatively high before the intervention.

Rothbaum et al. (2006) implemented a VRET application for the treatment of fear of flying. They showed a long-term decrease in flying-related anxiety with participants continuing to fly six and twelve months after the treatment. The study included 75 participants. The entry criteria of the experiment was a diagnosed specific phobia of the situational type, a panic disorder with agoraphobia or agoraphobia. The participants had to complete questionnaires at four different times (pre, post, 6-month after, 12-month after). The comparison of both, VRET and real-life exposure therapy, showed a decrease in anxiety right after the treatment and the BAT, the measure whether participants would avoid getting on a plane and fly was low for each condition in the follow-up measures. However, various limitations of the study are discussed, such as the generalizability of their results to a more diverse group of participants as well as the difficulty comparing both VR and real-life exposure as the experiences ultimately differ.

Regarding the VRET treatment of acrophobia, the fear of heights, Emmelkamp et al. (2002) developed a low-budget design, which entails a virtual environment with differing heights. While there was no control condition implemented, Emmelkamp et al. (2002) were able to show the effectiveness of the VRET application in comparison to in-vivo treatments, despite a reported low-effort implementation of the virtual environment. During the exposure, the patients' therapist was always around, controlling the program. Additionally, Rimer et al. (2021) generated a VRET application for acrophobia to improve clinicians' attitudes towards VRET and were able to initially induce discomfort within the participants during the exposure in VR similarly to real heights and enhance their attitudes after repeated use.

Difede et al. (2007) developed a VRET application for the treatment of *Post-Traumatic Stress Disorder* (PTSD), specifically related to the hijacking of planes, which were flown into the Twin Towers of the World Trade Center in New York on the 11th of September in 2001. Entry criteria for participants included the direct exposure to the attacks, and the diagnosis of PTSD. There were five people who had undergone previous though ineffective treatment that were assigned to the experimental condition. The virtual environment showed a virtual recreation of the events of the 11th of September. Participants attended an average of eight exposure sessions each lasting 45 minutes over at least six weeks of VRET. During the exposure, a therapist was present, encouraging the participants to verbally recount the traumatic event. The results showed a decrease in stress levels and participants maintained the improved values even after a six-month follow-up questionnaire.

VR is further utilized for the treatment of other mental disorders, such as anorexia nervosa (see Mölbert et al., 2018) or social phobia (see Roy et al., 2003). Various researchers have attempted to investigate the effectiveness of VR treatments through meta- analyses. Krijn et al. (2004), investigated the deployment of VRET for claustrophobia, fear of driving, acrophobia, fear of flying, spider phobia, fear of public speaking, panic disorder with agoraphobia, and PTSD. They suggested VRET to be an effective approach in comparison to no treatment, specifically for the treatment of specific phobias, fear of flying and acrophobia. However, they pointed out that VRET as a stand-alone treatment requires further research. Utilizing VRET is a cost-effective approach compared to the necessary resources of, for instance, having to take a flight in a therapy session. Moreover, Parsons and Rizzo (2008) observed 21 studies with a total of 300 participants and ascertained the decrease of anxiety symptoms following the use of a VRET application with a large effect size ($d = 0.95$). Additionally, Powers and Emmelkamp (2008), investigated 13 studies with a total of 397 participants, using VRET specifically for the treatment of anxiety disorders and showed a large mean effect size for VRET treatments ($d = 1.11$) and even a slight advantage compared to in-vivo treatments. Lastly, Morina et al. (2015) explored 14 clinical trials treating specific phobias and suggested that participants that participated in the VRET measure did not only perform significantly better than patients on a waitlist but also showed comparable results to in-vivo treatments.

The mentioned researchers have shown the different types of existing VR studies and the effectiveness of VR to treat mental disorders, which establishes it as an appropriate alternative or addition to regular therapy. It not only allows precise control and manipulation, but also relief of mental health care professionals. However, as Krijn et al. (2004) mentioned, VRET as a stand-alone treatment is still in its infancy. Many studies using VRET have mentioned a therapist to be present during the intervention, and the virtual environment solely functioning as the exposure stimulus. The relevance of the bond between patients and their therapists has been shown in many studies, thus the effects on the outcome of the treatment should not be neglected. But what if the virtual environment could not only display the exposure stimulus but also allow the virtual embodiment of a therapist?

2.3 The Role of Therapist-Patient bond, Virtual Agents and Embodied AI

The relationship between the patient and the therapist is crucial as it should be built on trust to establish a safe environment for the patients to discuss their struggles and incorporate their therapist's input into their lives. A few studies have addressed the effect of a therapist's behavior and the therapist-patient bond on the success of the therapeutic intervention. While this varies among different types of treatment, Luborsky et al. (1985) suggest that interpersonal differences in patients' characteristics did not explain any variance in therapy success. Moreover, an early measure of patient- therapist relationship showed a significant correlation with therapy outcomes. Parish and Eagle (2003) emphasize the *alliance*, i.e., the bond with one's therapist to be of considerable importance and strongly affects the outcome of a therapeutic treatment. Consequently, a higher alliance can have positive outcomes on treatment success. Høglend (2014) discussed the role of *transference* in therapist-patient relationship, meaning the transfer of previous experiences onto current situations and persons. He addressed the practice of alliance-focused treatment, wherein there was a special focus on the bond between therapist and patient and the therapist, for instance, practices more self-disclosure. The bond between therapist and patient can therefore positively affect a patient's healing journey. However, as noted above, the available therapists are unable to carry the number of people affected, and although the effectiveness of VRET is evident, if every encounter requires therapeutic supervision, it fails to provide the full extent of accessibility that VRET applications allow. So how can a similar power be provided in the context of VR, and how can the therapeutic bond be mimicked without requiring the availability of a human therapist?

Mechanisms, such as the *Media Equation* or the *Computers are Social Actors* (CASA) paradigm suggest that technological systems are treated like a human counterpart, i.e., the same interpersonal cues are applied in human-technology interaction as they are in human-human interaction (Nass et al., 1994; Reeves & Nass, 1996). Research with *Intelligent Virtual Agents* (IVA) shows the possibility of inducing empathy towards an IVA, e.g., through ingroup cues (Obremski et al., 2023; Paiva et al., 2017). The virtual embodiment is rather common and has come up in many different contexts (e.g., Tamborini et al., 2018). However, most studies deploy a Wizard-Of-Oz logic, which entails a costly and time-consuming development to enable the selection of buttons and audio samples. Therefore, it is not very flexible and thus potentially decreases the level of personalization and quality of the interaction. Specifically, for the deployment of IVAs in VRET applications, the Wizard-Of-Oz concept is not feasible. Utilizing *embodied conversational agents* (or embodied AI), i.e., virtual agents connected to AI allows the possibility of dynamic and personalized interaction, and the possibility of providing the AI with guidelines and information around the therapeutic intervention beforehand.

2.4 What is Artificial Intelligence?

Understanding AI is crucial for implementing applications in the treatment of mental disorders. AI can be separated into two parts: *artificial* and *intelligence.* The term artificial refers to something that is created by human beings and does not occur naturally (Oxford University Press, 2025a), whereas intelligence is defined as the capacity to understand, learn and apply knowledge (Oxford University Press, 2025b). Hence, AI is broadly understood as the human-made ability to process information and thus mimic certain aspects of the cognition and behaviour of human beings.

Scientific literature reflects a variety of different definitions. Kok et al. (2009), for instance, discuss the difficulty of finding a single, over-arching definition for AI. They suggest AI to be better understood as 'artificially intelligent systems' (p. 271) capable of both the ability to imitate thoughts and actions of human beings as well as the skill to act in a rational manner. Russell and Norvig (2016) support the agent-like nature of AI, primarily characterized as systems that receive information from the environment, process this data using complex algorithms, and produce an output in the form of, e.g., an action, an image or video or text. Regulatory guidelines have been adopted more recently to regulate the deployment of safe AI-systems in the European Union. The European AI Act, introduced in March of 2024, defines AI as a 'machine-based system that is designed to operate with varying levels of autonomy' and which generates 'outputs such as predictions, content, recommendations, or decisions that can influence physical or virtual environments' (European Parliament, 2024, Art. 3(1)). The AI Act addresses further aspects of AI, i.e., the involvement of machinery, the consequences for the environment it interacts with, and the different levels of self-determination of systems.

Within the broad field of AI, various subfields are of importance. *Machine Learning* (ML) represents one of the essential components. ML techniques, often derived from models inspired by human neural networks, involve feeding large datasets into algorithms and enabling the system to generate predictions about future input through utilizing different methods, for example, labelling of data, i.e., *Supervised Learning* (Murdoch et al., 2019). Additionally, ML incorporates methods for interpreting its own output, thus enhancing the system's performance over time. Another crucial domain is *Natural Language Processing* (NLP). NLP utilizes deep learning techniques to analyse complex language patterns and generate human language. This enables AI systems to not only understand natural language produced by its users, but also the generation of intelligible output, which is crucial when deploying AI in interactive applications (Raparthi et al., 2021). Considering the amount of different use cases AI is deployed in, the systems are trained on large sets of data, i.e., *Large Language Models* (LLM), such as the state-of-the-art *Generative Pre-trained Transformer* (GPT) model, which allows coherent context-specific responses (Brown et al., 2020). The Transformer architecture was developed by a team of Google employees and applies an attention mechanism, which helps the model weigh the importance of different words rather than applying a recurrent structure and can therefore be applicable to tasks it was not explicitly trained on (Vaswani et al., 2017).

The interactive component of AI is further highlighted in the field *AI-Mediated Communication*. Hancock et al. (2020) discuss a latitude of AI intervention in interpersonal communication, which reaches from minimal modifications like in text improvement, to fully autonomously generated messages aimed at achieving intended conversational goals. The deployment of autonomous AI-systems has allowed the efficient sourcing of otherwise time-consuming tasks, such as detecting misinformation (Demartini et al., 2020), enhancing customer service (Buhalis & Moldasvska, 2022; Khan & Iqbal, 2020), and facilitating the recruiting process (Lacroux & Lacroux, 2022). The various fields AI is deployed in with increasing amounts of autonomy to act with less and less human intervention, is accompanied by risks and concerns that need to be put into consideration. The following section aims at giving a rough overview of possible challenges that might arise in the deployment of AI.

2.5 Risks of Artificial Intelligence

With rising awareness about sustainable living and decreasing one's carbon footprint, the environmental risks of AI have not gone unnoticed. Whilst AI can, for instance, contribute to improving a company's sustainable policy, the deployment of AI itself uses up a considerable amount of carbon emissions. This has brought upon various research efforts to encourage a more environmentally friendly approach from hardware to training to usage (Gaur et al., 2023; Wu et al., 2022). Moreover, the rapid development of AI-systems has consequences of economic nature and has triggered a change in the workforce. But how likely are the prevalent concerns of AI taking over one's job? Around 75% of businesses are predicted to adopt the technology of AI into their workflow by 2027 (Statista, 2023). Therefore, the benefits of implementing AI are apparent for companies worldwide, such as supporting employees to meet the growing demands of globalization. While the loss of around 83 million jobs—with the distribution depending on the field of work—is expected in the upcoming years, AI is also predicted to elicit the creation of an additional 69 million jobs through re-structuring of the work force (LitsLink, 2024).

Aside from organizational difficulties, the development and usage of AI-systems additionally leaves room for error. As pointed out above, AI-systems are trained on big data sets, which entail knowledge and information generated in previous years. Considering the changes and advancements that have happened within society throughout the past decades alone, amplifying previous, possibly outdated information, which might entail biased data can have serious consequences. Kordzadeh and Ghasemaghaei (2021) have reviewed relevant literature from different databases regarding bias in AI-systems from 2010 to 2019 and have identified the term *algorithmic bias*, i.e., bias rooted within the AI's training data. Whereas they point out the difficulty of finding one over-arching definition to clarify the meaning of algorithmic bias, each definition inherently exhibits the inequal treatment of individuals and the repeated occurrence thereof. In turn, this can result in the amplification of already existing inequalities within society, such as higher prediction of crimes in areas more densely populated by minorities. A now discontinued hiring tool developed by Amazon utilizing AI, for instance, has shown the consequences of algorithmic bias through hiring fewer female staff in manager positions (Dastin, 2022). The tool has presumably been fed with information on current employees and previous hiring decisions. The failure of such a tool can allow for the reflection on previous recruiting decisions and elicit a more diversified pool of employees as well as adjustment of recruiting tools. However, its deployment could lead to the discrimination of social groups or minorities, based on their race, gender, religious beliefs or socio-economic status (Panch et al., 2019). Apart from algorithmic bias, i.e., bias rooted in the AI's training data, Danks and London (2017) have identified additional types of biases occurring in autonomous AI like the bias arising if an application is employed outside its intended use, i.e., *transfer context bias*, and *interpretation bias*, caused by the misinterpretation of algorithmic output. Therefore, it is crucial to differentiate between the nature of a bias when intending to identify or prevent the occurrence thereof. Ultimately, Kordzadeh and Ghasemaghaei (2021) emphasize the prioritization of people's well-being when designing AI.

Furthermore, whilst AI can facilitate many tasks, like finding ideas for a romantic date, writing an essay or even summarizing a scientific paper, it has repeatedly been found to *hallucinate* information. Hallucinating in the context of AI is understood as the generation of false information or providing non-existent sources and thus enabling the spreading of misinformation (Monteith et al., 2024). As its priority is to interact with the user as naturally as possible and adequately fulfil requests, it can often lead to output that eventually might cause harm. The AI's output has increasingly improved so much so that mechanisms must be put in place to decipher *Deep Fakes*, i.e., images, video or audio outputs, which closely replicate, for example, celebrities from real imagery (Yang et al., 2019). Such faults can not only inflict psychological but also physical harm, for instance, in autonomous driving systems (Brell et al., 2019). Taking into consideration the world of *Big Data* (Chen et al., 2014) and the quantity of data shared, another big risk that has been vastly discussed, is the safety of data exchanged in the interaction with an AI model. Consequently, the level of agency the AI should obtain has been questioned, specifically, in the mental health context, which primarily requires the transfer of sensitive medical data.

2.6 Artificial Intelligence in Mental Health Care

As discussed before, mental health plays an important role in an individual's health and the general maintenance of a functioning society. Germany's Council of Experts addresses the general deployment of AI-based systems in health care to mitigate the shortage of skilled professionals, e.g., through monitoring the movement of people in need of care and alarm personnel accordingly or the efficient analysis of patients' medical data (Sachverständigenrat, 2024). In mental health care, AI allows the diagnosis of mental disorders or the improvement of personalized therapy approaches through the fast analysis of datasets as well as monitoring a person's well-being through voice or physiological measures, such as heart rate (D'Alfonso, 2020). Particularly with the no-contact guidelines put in place during the Covid-19 pandemic, AI-powered conversational text-based chatbots have gained popularity. Woebot Health, for instance, provides the conversational app Woebot, which is specifically designed to give users chat-based support regarding topics around mental health. Their own analysis shows a 24% reduction in burnout on their website; a pilot study suggests a reduction in symptoms of mild depression in athletes after continued usage (Qi, 2024). The chatbot Wysa elicited a higher improvement in symptoms of depression for more frequent users compared to less frequent users (Inkster et al., 2018). Additionally, Replika developed by the company Luka in San Francisco is another AI-based empathetic companion, advertised to care and listen.

The advancements of AI are further applied for many mental health care tools in the background. For example, Quartet Health deploys ML to connect patients with suitable professionals to ensure appropriate and personalized therapy treatments through their platform. AI is also employed to analyse text-based communication sent to the American Crisis Text Line to determine individuals in need of immediate support (Crisis Text Line, 2018). Furthermore, Wearables based on AI-systems allow the tracking of sleep patterns and heart rate to track stress levels and support an individual's overall well-being (Sleep Review Magazine, 2023). MindStrong, a mental health company that has since gone out of business, started out tracking users' interaction with their smartphones to detect early signs of depression through e.g., tracking typing speed. Similarly, AI depression detectors (AIDD) have been developed to track early signs of depression on social media (Laacke et al., 2021).

It is important to note that whilst there are various forms of technologies available to provide mental health support, research regarding the effectiveness of such applications happens at a delay and often fails to reflect the mass of inventions. While the deployment of AI has many advantages for mental health care, treatment approaches such as exposure therapy are further enhanced through the deployment of VR as outlined before. Although mental health is not solely defined by the absence of mental disorders, this work focuses primarily on mental health disorders and the possibility of using VR and AI for the treatment thereof.

Ultimately, there are various risks and ethical concerns that need to be considered when deploying AI in combination with VR to provide an encompassing technological approach for the treatment of mental disorders. As research regarding AI and VR use for mental health care is progressing quickly, many ethical implications have been formulated to establish a safe implementation of AI, which is crucial to consider before the development to avoid harmful behaviour.

2.7 Ethical Implications for the Use of AI and VR in Mental Health Care

While many studies have already shown the effectiveness of VRET applications and various AI-based tools are already being used in mental health care, the risks associated with the use of these new technologies and the possibility of harmful behavior and failure to achieve the desired treatment outcome, remain. To ensure the safety of users interacting with these new technologies, a variety of ethical principles were formulated. Ethics encompass the general regulation of people's behaviour based on certain principles with the aim of creating a safe environment (Aguinis & Henle, 2004). In Germany, the Ethic's Council oversees ethical issues and provides guidance to companies and organizations. While they elaborate on an ethical handling of sensitive data when utilizing new technologies and the importance of data safety and risk avoidance, which is specifically relevant in mental health care, they also emphasise the advancements of AI and encourage its usage (Ethikrat, 2023). Moreover, Kuhn et al. (2009) emphasize the thorough analysis of each treatment approach regarding risks and benefits of the intervention. Consequently, Obremski and Wienrich (2024) summarized five over-arching ethical principles relevant for the development and deployment of AI (and VR) in mental health care. The five main ethical principles are: **Beneficence, Risk Avoidance, Autonomy, Fairness** and **Involvement.**

The principle of **Beneficence** entails both the concept of unbiasedness and forming trust. This addresses the importance of the previously discussed bond between therapist and patient as well as the risks accompanied by biased AI-system. The realization of beneficence in VRET applications and embodied AI can be facilitated through the type of embodiment, like the level of naturalness of speech and the implementation of ingroup cues, e.g., same gender as the user or similar background and characteristics (Obremski et al., 2023). To ensure unbiased algorithms, a particular attention to type of data used for training is pointed out. The disregard of this principle could interfere with the effectiveness of the therapeutic treatment and potentially worsen symptoms through enforcing negative stereotypes (see Kordzadeh & Ghasemaghaei, 2021).

The second principle of **Risk Avoidance** addresses the importance of preventing and navigating harmful behaviour of the AI-system. The risk assessment differentiates between a therapy approach, which includes a therapist in the treatment, i.e., *therapist-in- the-loop* and the possibility of a stand-alone treatment, i.e., *therapist-out-of-the-loop.* Disregarding the concept of **Risk Avoidance** might cause physical and psychological harm to patients through unpredictable behaviour of implemented systems. Thus, it is proposed that systems used in mental health care should be held to a similar standard as mental health care professionals and follow-up sessions should be incorporated (Fiske et al., 2019). The implication Fiske et al. (2019) discussed in this regard is the supervision of tools by trained mental health care professionals and the adherence to set guidelines, like referencing appropriate services.

The third principle of **Autonomy** covers the widely discussed risk of data security in the interaction with AI and the relevance of providing users with autonomy over their own data, which is particularly important when handling sensitive medical data as it can lead to embarrassment and make patients vulnerable in other areas, e.g., when applying for a job. Therefore, Obremski and Wienrich (2024) additionally point out the need for transparency about the processing of collected sensitive information and informed consent.

The accessibility of information and facilitating the understanding of AI regardless of one's educational background is described within the fourth principle of **Fairness**. It points out the importance of therapists and patients knowing how the application works and urges to incorporate this in the design process. This principle underlines the importance of encouraging *AI literacy*, i.e., 'a set of competencies that enables individuals to critically evaluate AI technologies, communicate and collaborate effectively with AI, and use AI' (Long & Magerko, 2020, p. 2).

The final ethical principle of **Involvement** is addressed by Tavory (2024) as she emphasized the importance of human involvement. The risks of AI taking jobs and replacing qualified personnel are considered in various areas where AI is deployed. However, the **Involvement** aspect emphasizes the importance of including therapeutic personnel in the design process and applying their expertise to improve applications. Furthermore, it allows a variety of new tools, which with the help of experienced therapists can be used for new types of treatment and enhance therapy without replacing personnel (Fiske et al., 2019). Additionally, it could help reach populations that might not seek out professional help in the first place. Whereas the responsible AI approach is commonly supported and reflected in the prevalent ethical principles, Tavory (2024) argues that designing for responsible AI is not encompassing and should be expanded by the *Ethics of Care* perspective. The Ethics of Care additionally include the concept of affective computing and acknowledging the responsibility towards the people that are cared for, thus emphasises the focus on interpersonal relationships and preventing emotional manipulation.

In recent years, the concept of *human-centered AI* (HCAI) has gained popularity and is increasingly encouraged as the standard practice. It is an approach that places the human at the centre of design and evaluation of systems. This can be acquired by including users at an early stage of development and implementing users' ideas as well as accommodate their concerns (Auernhammer, 2020; Shneiderman, 2022). While there are a variety of different ethical implications, the vulnerability and perception of the patient is not at the centre, so it remains unclear, what concerns future users have, for instance, about the usage of an AI-controlled application to treat mental health disorders. As the effectiveness of VR treatments has been established through meta-analyses (Krijn et al., 2004; Morina et al., 2015), it is not guaranteed that patients affected by mental disorders intend to use these new technologies on a large-scale. Therefore, in line with the Ethics of Care perspective and HCAI approach it is important to determine the concerns patients have and navigate those in future design. Secondly, while Obremski & Wienrich (2024) have already indicated which technological implications arise from the postulated ethical guidelines, it is crucial to a) make the variety of abstract ethical implications more tangible to facilitate technological development and b) prioritize, what is most important in the direct and indirect interaction with the user. Consequently, an explorative pre-study aims to answer the following research question:

RQ1: What are the concerns of mental health patients regarding the use of AI and VR for the treatment of mental health disorders?

Gillespie et al. (2021) show the importance of data privacy and transparency and explainability for five countries, namely USA, Canada, Germany, UK and Australia when interacting with AI-systems. When setting the focus on HCAI, the ethical guidelines underline two principles, which are most relevant, yet easily manipulable: Data Autonomy and Transparency. Gillespie et al. (2021) additionally argue that a relevant factor of effective and meaningful interaction with AI is perceived trust towards the AI system.

Moreover, trust in turn affects self-disclosure, which is of high relevance when designing AI-systems for the treatment of mental disorders. Therefore, the following paragraphs discuss the relevance of autonomy and transparency for self-disclosure and trust towards the AI, and thus the hypotheses for this study are explained.

2.8 The Role of Privacy, Data Protection Laws and Autonomy

Legal guidelines, such as the German Act to Accelerate the Digitalisation of Healthcare, which was passed in March 2024, aim to advance the health care system with the more frequent use of technology e.g., for cancer research (Ekinci, 2023). The Health Data Use Act (GDNG, Gesundheitsdatennutzungsgesetz) regulates the use of medical data and aims to facilitate the accessibility of patient information, i.a., for research (Bundesministerium der Justiz, 2024; Bundesministerium für Gesundheit, 2023). While this allows advancements in health care and the possibility for new treatment approaches, it also requires the adaptation of existing data protection laws, considering the handling of sensitive medical data. In addition to the General Data Protection Regulation (GDPR), the European Union enforced the *EU AI Act* in August 2024, which aims at regulating the use of AI, sorting AI applications into three different risk categories: unacceptable risk (banned), high-risk applications and unregulated risk. Moreover, it restricts its use and development accordingly (European Parliament, 2024).

On the 15th of January 2025, Germany introduced a nation-wide electronic patient file (ePA, 'elektronische Patientenakte'), which entails the creation of a digital file of every patient's data unless they explicitly object, thereby adhering to an 'opt-out' approach opposed to the hitherto prevalent 'opt-in' solution, which required an active agreement of data usage (Bundesärztekammer, 2024). Leading up to the introduction of the ePA, many interviews were conducted to examine attitudes regarding this innovation, suggesting that most people are concerned about the safety of their medical data and doubt the usefulness of the system with specifically the passive agreement being criticized (AOK Presse und Politik, 2024; Deloitte Deutschland, 2024; Reinecke et al., 2008).

In Obremski and Wienrich (2024) the principle of Autonomy regarding data has already come up. Moreover, the EU AI Act emphasizes the importance of remaining autonomous, with humans having the final say on AI-controlled decisions. But what role does autonomy play for human beings? In the Self-Determination Theory (SDT) autonomy is described as a central psychological need, which includes the control to act in alignment with one's values (Deci & Ryan, 2012). Fulfilling this need shows to be crucial for an individual's well-being, and thus mental health. Therefore, this study aims at researching the importance of data autonomy in the interaction with an embodied AI in the context of a therapeutic consultation, to design responsible AI (see Calvo et al., 2020).

Privacy and control over one's data is described as a relevant aspect of acting and perceiving oneself as an autonomous individual (Kupfer, 1987). Norberg et al. (2007) described the differences in intended data disclosure and actual disclosure of personal information, i.e. the *'privacy paradox'*, showing that many individuals tend to share more of their own data than initially intended. It is additionally pointed out that there is an important difference in types of data with sensitive data posing a higher risk e.g., of later causing embarrassment for the involved party or feeling as though one is giving parts of themselves away. Petronio (quoted by Margulis, 2011) developed the theory of the *Communication Privacy Management* (CPM) in which he describes a rule-based management system that is supposed to determine the factors that influence individuals in how they share personal or private information. Among other propositions, he postulates that individuals perceive themselves to have the right to not only be in control of who should receive ownership over their information but more importantly, how third parties should manage the ownership of their data. While this theory describes implicit aspects of data disclosure, there are various external factors that influence the distribution of personal information. As the aim is to utilize embodied AI for the treatment of mental health disorders, self-disclosure of patients is very important in providing efficient and personalized treatment. *Self-disclosure* is understood as sharing something about oneself that was previously unknown, which can significantly affect the bond between two people. As not each disclosure of information about the self is of the same effect, there are different types of information that can be shared about oneself, such as biographic data or attitudes as well as fears and personal beliefs (Joinson & Paine, 2007). Self-disclosure appears to be higher when anonymity is granted, for example, in computer-mediated interaction. However, this is specifically the case when interacting through text-based communication (Joinson et al., 2010). WheandP2reas interaction with an embodied AI in VR grants a level of anonymity, yet requires face-to-face communication, it would be interesting to see how much individuals disclose in AI-mediated communication in a therapy context. Research has shown virtual avatars to elicit higher self- disclosure for higher socially anxious people (Kang & Gratch, 2010), and the disclosure of more sensitive topics (Pickard et al., 2016) compared to the interaction with a real human. Moreover, the risk of social judgment strongly affects the amount of self-disclosure, therefore, there has been higher observed self-disclosure with an AI as the AI-mediated communication elicits less perceived judgment (Kim et al., 2021). These findings further support the use of AI in mental health care.

The importance of privacy on personal data disclosure has been established and in turn the relevance of control or autonomy of the collection and distribution. Taddei and Contena (2013) pointed out the impact of privacy concerns and perceived risks on self- disclosure. Considering the formulation of the ethical principle of Data Autonomy and the resulting control users are provided over how their data is collected and transferred, it is hypothesized that an increase in autonomy will also result in an increase in users' self- disclosure. Consequently, the following first hypothesis is formulated as following:

H1: The condition with higher **autonomy** regarding one's data results in higher **self- disclosure** compared to the legal condition.

There have been various research efforts underlining the relationship of trust and the amount of presented self-disclosure (Joinson et al., 2010; Steel, 1991; Wheeless & Grotz, 1977). Lee et al. (2024) examined rapport with a text-based AI-chatbot in the psychotherapy context and its influence on self-disclosure. This research showed a mediating positive effect of the perceived bond to the AI-chatbot on fear of negative evaluation and therefore increased the amount of self-disclosure. As pointed out previously, trust is a crucial factor in fostering the patient-therapist relationship. Therefore, trust is considered to have a moderating factor on the relationship between autonomy and self-disclosure, postulating that lower or higher trust towards the AI might consequently alter the relationship between autonomy and self-disclosure respectively (see Fig. 2.1).

H2: The amount of **trust towards the AI** moderates the strength of the relationship between **autonomy** and the amount of **self-disclosure**.

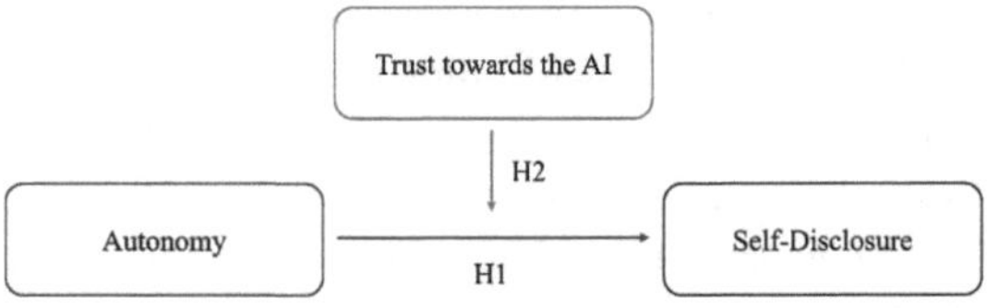

Fig. 2.1 The moderating effect of trust on the relationship between autonomy and self-disclosure

2.9 The Role of Transparency for Trust and Self-Disclosure

The debate around transparency has been further reinforced with the discussions around network neutrality when various telecommunications companies were revealed to block or delay certain traffic online, which led to the Net Neutrality Guideline introduced through the European Union (Abiteboul & Stoyanovich, 2019; Laoutaris, 2018). Therefore, extensive research efforts have been made around the concept of *Explainable AI* (XAI) as opposed to the common perception of AI as an incomprehensible 'black box' (Minh et al., 2022; Samek & Müller, 2019). XAI incorporates different aspects, with the over-arching themes addressing transparency, interpretability and explainability (Angelov et al., 2021). As this work focuses on HCAI in the use of mental health care, the direct user interaction is altered through increasing the transparency about the functions and data collection by the AI. Danks and London (2017) have addressed different types of algorithmic biases, such as the *interpretation bias*, which occurs when the output is misinterpreted. This bias might be mitigated by providing more context about the manipulation of the AI to appropriately interpret the AI's output. Additionally, transparency addresses the ethical concept of **Fairness** and contributes to a better understanding of AI in mental health care. Research suggests that the perceived informativeness about a subject matter can determine the extent to which personal data is shared (Smink et al., 2019). Based on findings regarding the impact of different factors on self-disclosure reported above, the third hypothesis is formulated (see Figure 2):

H3: The condition with higher **transparency** regarding the AI's function and data protection results in higher **self-disclosure** compared to the legal condition.

Regarding algorithmic bias Kordzadeh and Ghasemaghaei (2021) pointed out that providing transparency can increase users' trust. Liu (2021) showed that when interacting with AI on a website, informative transparency regarding the AI's function resulted in higher trust compared to the condition with placebic transparency. Shin (2020) suggested that users perceive AI to be more trustworthy when its decisions appear more transparent and explainable. Glikson and Woolley (2020) conducted a review of research on trust in AI and reinforce the relevance of transparency for trust in virtual AI. However, they also expressed the importance of long-term effects of transparency on trust and the differentiation of types of trust, such as emotional trust. Wienrich and Obremski (2024) implemented transparency cues and suggest the congruency with other presented framing, in their study expert-framing, to increase trust towards the AI. Whereas their manipulated transparency cues had little effect, perceived transparency showed to predict trust. Considering the presented findings, a fourth hypothesis is formulated (see Fig. 2.2):

H4: The condition with higher **transparency** regarding the AI's function and data protection results in higher **trust towards the AI** compared to the legal condition.

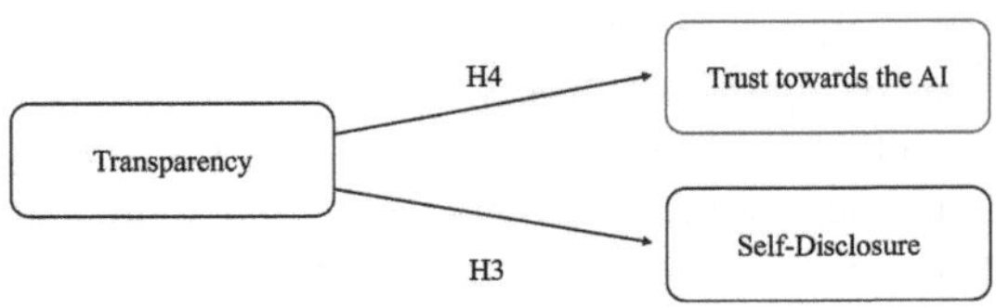

Fig. 2.2 A visual representation of H3 and H4 for the manipulation of transparency

The effects of autonomy deduced from the SDT suggest higher positive affect by providing users with increased control (see Jeno et al., 2019). Moreover, Kallinen (2017) showed that increased transparency through providing feedback decreased stress, i.e., negative affect within the participants. These findings indicate the effect of autonomy and transparency on positive affect, which is formulated in the fifth hypothesis:

H5: The two conditions with higher **autonomy** and higher **transparency** result in higher positive affect compared to the legal condition.

The overall aim of the implemented virtual environment and embodied AI set up may eventually be used for the treatment of anxiety disorders. Considering the importance of transparency and autonomy as ethical principles in AI in mental health care, a final hypothesis regarding their effect on perceived safety at an exposure level for acrophobia, i.e., a terrace in VR is postulated:

H6: The two conditions with higher **autonomy** and higher **transparency** lead to higher perceived safety with the embodied AI at the exposure level compared to the legal condition.

The following sections describe the measures of the pre-study, the resulting implementation of the main study and the measures of the main study.

Pre-Study 3

The following section discusses the pre-study including measures, results and discussion of results, followed by a conclusion and implications for the main study.

3.1 Measures

The measures section provides an overview of implemented scales as well as self-created items and open questions to gain the intended insights regarding concerns about usage and data transfer when using AI and VR in a therapy context.

3.1.1 Screening and Participants

Within the pre-study an online questionnaire through the participant collection online tool Prolific was conducted, allowing the controlled selection of suitable participants. To only include possible future users, participants were pre-screened with the following filters (see Prolific, 2024):

➜ 'Location' – Germany
➜ 'Health – Mental Health Diagnosis: Are you currently diagnosed with a mental health condition?' – Yes

Supplementary Information The online version contains supplementary material available at https://doi.org/10.1007/978-3-658-50067-2_3.

P. Friedrich, *To be healed or to be hacked*, BestMasters,
https://doi.org/10.1007/978-3-658-50067-2_3

The two above listed filters first ensured that all participants understood the questionnaire that was entirely in German. Secondly, it included any person diagnosed with a mental health condition, not just anxiety disorders or depression as this allowed a bigger pool of eligible participants. Within the questionnaire, a short video of the application described in Obremski and Wienrich (2024) utilized for the treatment of acrophobia is presented, showing its procedure and different steps. Therefore, participants' answers are directly applicable to the specific purpose of the application and future development can include further precautions.

The online questionnaire was conducted through the website Prolific between 17.12.2024 and 18.12.2024. Participants received an average payment of 9 pounds per hour and the participation took an average of 15 minutes. The participants were between 18 and 66 years old (M = 32.03, SD = 10.16). Of the N = 152 participants n = 80 (52.6%) were female, n = 66 (43.4%) were male and n = 5 (3.3%) were diverse and one person (0.7%) selected 'others'. Participants indicated a variety of different education levels, namely n = 5 (3.3%) participants have a Hauptschulabschluss (Secondary school leaving certificate), n = 19 (12.5%) Mittlere Reife (Intermediate school leaving certificate), n = 39 (25.7%) Allgemeine Hochschulreife/Abitur (A-levels), n = 9 (5.9%) Fachabitur (Technical baccalaureate), n = 23 (15.1%) finished their apprenticeship, n = 34 (22.4%) have a Bachelor's degree and n = 20 (13.2%) have a Master's degree as well as n = 3 (2.0%) have a docorate. A total of n = 122 (80.3%) participants selected German to be their mother tongue, whereas n = 30 (19.7%) participants specified their mother tongue to be something else, precisely: one person (0.7%) each indicated Armenian, Bosnian, Georgian, Hungarian, Persian and Portuguese to be their mother tongue. 2 (1.3%) people indicated their mother tongue to be Ukrainian, 3 people (2.0%) each listed to be Russian and Spanish, 4 participants (2.6%) were Polish, 5 (3.3%) English and 7 (4.6%) Turkish.

3.1.2 Procedure of the study

Every participant fulfilling the above-mentioned criteria (location Germany, diagnosed with a mental disorder), was granted access to the questionnaire. In Prolific they were transferred to the SosciSurvey website and started the questionnaire. At the beginning a brief text described the purpose and content of the study, which was followed by information regarding the collection of their data, including the participants' right to have their collected data deleted at any point without explanation, that their participation is voluntary, and their data remains anonymous as well as the information about the regulatory agency responsible. Participants were asked whether they agreed to the collection of their data and wanted to participate in the study. Participants were able to object to the usage of their data and were thus excluded from the participation and directly forwarded to the final page of the questionnaire. To ensure easy data deletion and the allocation of the respective cases without violating anonymization, participants were additionally asked to create a codeword based on numbers, such as their own date of birth or the number of letters of their mother's first name.

Participants were then asked to state some of their demographic data, such as age, gender, language, level of education and mother tongue. Furthermore, participants were queried about their personal disposition regarding affinity for technology, trust disposition, items about trust and data security, privacy attitudes and informativeness about the use of AI in therapy. After this, a short explanation of 'exposure therapy' was given, followed by a 1.30-minute-long video, showing the procedure of the implemented application and the talking AI therapist. The 'Next' button of the questionnaire was manipulated to only be displayed after 90 seconds spent on the page to ensure participants read the text and watched the video thoroughly. Following the video, there were various questions regarding attitudes about personal data in health care, the perceived eeriness of the depicted agent in the video, preferences of different therapy types, attitudes about AI use in therapy and the assessment of the importance of different factors. Additionally, two open questions about concerns regarding the transfer of personal data and the use of VR therapy with AI were presented. Lastly, participants were debriefed about the purpose of the study and thanked for their participation as well as provided with a link and a code to verify their participation within Prolific.

3.1.3 Affinity for Technology Interaction, Trust and Privacy Attitudes Questionnaire

After the demographic data, the Affinity for technology interaction (ATI) scale by Franke et al. (2019) was used, consisting of nine items, namely: 'I like to occupy myself in greater detail with technical systems.', 'I like testing the functions of new technical systems.', 'I predominantly deal with technical systems because I have to.', 'When I have a new technical system in front of me, I try it out intensively.', 'I enjoy spending time becoming acquainted with a new technical system.', 'It is enough for me that a technical system works; I don't care how or why.', 'I try to understand how a technical system exactly works.', 'It is enough for me to know the basic functions of a technical system.' and 'I try to make full use of the capabilities of a technical system.'. Cronbach's alpha was calculated to assess the internal consistency of the ATI scale, which showed a high consistency with $\alpha = .92$.

To assess the participants' general ability to trust, the Propensity to trust subscale of the Scale of Online Trust (SCOUT) developed by Bär et al. (2011) was employed, using three items: 'It's easy for me to trust people or things.', 'I tend to trust people or things quickly.' and 'I find it difficult to trust someone. (recoded)'. The three items showed a high internal consistency of $\alpha = .92$.

Additionally, participants' general trust towards technology and data security was measured using the scale developed by Backhaus (2011). The subscale trust and data security was used and the two subscales trust and reputation were excluded as they did not appear necessary for the purpose of this study. The used scale showed a high internal consistency of $\alpha = .95$. The wording of the scale was adjusted to fit the use of AI. The subscale consists of eleven items and participants were asked to assess their attitudes regarding the following statements about AI (e.g., ChatGPT, voice assistants): 'I think Artificial Intelligence makes an effort to protect the privacy of its users.', 'I feel safe when I send personal data to an Artificial Intelligence.', 'I think Artificial Intelligence complies with data protection laws.', 'I think Artificial Intelligence only collects personal data from its users when it is really necessary.', 'I think Artificial Intelligence respects the rights of its users when retrieving personal data.', 'I think that Artificial Intelligence does not pass on my personal data to third parties.', 'I think Artificial Intelligence uses mechanisms for secure data transmission.', 'I think Artificial Intelligence is very concerned about the security of data transmission.', 'When I send data to an Artificial Intelligence, I am sure that the data cannot be intercepted by third parties.', 'I think that Artificial Intelligence protects my data from malicious access by third parties.' and 'Overall, I think an Artificial Intelligence is a safe place for sensitive information.'. There was an attention check included, namely 'Please select 'fully agree'.' to ensure participants read through the items thoroughly and did not randomly click through them.

The Privacy Attitudes Questionnaire (PAQ) by Chignell et al. (2003) was used to assess participants' general attitudes towards privacy. For this study, the two subscales 'Interest in protection (P)' with eight items and 'Willingness to share personal information (PI)' with ten items were deployed, which were all translated into German. The items for the P scale are as follows: 'I would prefer to have an unlisted phone number.', 'I like to clear my cache frequently for privacy reasons.', 'I like to change my passwords frequently.', 'I like to close my curtains at home at night.', 'I frequently question why I'm providing personal information.', 'I would prefer people to knock before coming into my office or bedroom.',

'I worry about the possibility that my conversations will be overheard.', 'I would use a personal firewall.'. The items for the PI scale were as follows: 'I am comfortable with giving a DNA sample.', 'I am comfortable giving out my personal identification number.', 'I am comfortable in allowing others to check my credit.', 'I am comfortable wearing a name tag.', 'Employers should be able to monitor employee email.', 'It is ok to use messaging services even if the messages could in principle be tracked.', 'I allow strangers to enter my house while I'm not there.', 'I am comfortable with having my retina scanned.', 'I do not mind using my real name in online discussions.' and 'My medical information should never be communicated to people or organizations without my permission. (recoded)'. Lastly, a single self-created item was used to assess participants' informedness regarding research on AI for health care: 'How would you rate your knowledge of current research into the use of Artificial Intelligence in healthcare?'.

The P subscale with 8 items shows an acceptable internal consistency of $\alpha = .67$, whereas the PI subscale with 9 items has an internal consistency of $\alpha = .66$. All items were measured on a 7-point Likert scale reaching from 1 = 'do not agree at all' to 7 = 'fully agree'.

3.1.4 Perception of and Attitudes towards the Virtual Agent, AI and Data Security

To assess the participants' attitudes towards data security in health care, four items from the questionnaire created by the insurance company AOK Rheinland/ Hamburg (2024) in regard to the ePA were used: 'The right of access to health data is very important to me.', 'Data security is very important to me.', 'Improving emergency care is important to me.', 'I am concerned about the inadequate protection of my personal data.'.

Additionally, four self-created items were added regarding the sharing of one's personal data within health care when using AI: 'I would be willing to disclose my personal data to improve emergency care, e.g., for research purposes.', 'I have no concerns about entrusting my sensitive data to an AI.', 'I would feel more comfortable disclosing my data if I was informed exactly how my sensitive data would be used.' and 'I would feel more comfortable disclosing my data if I could determine exactly which of my data is stored.'. The internal consistency of the eight items was acceptable with $\alpha = .59$. To determine participants' general attitudes towards AI use in mental health care, seven self-created items were implemented with an internal consistency of $\alpha = .91$, which can be seen in Table 3.

Moreover, to also assess participants' preferences of therapy form, three items were included: 'Therapy with a human therapist is better than no therapy.', 'Therapy with an embodied AI is better than no therapy.' and 'Therapy with an embodied AI and the additional support of a human therapist is better than no therapy.' to be rated on a 7-point Likert scale reaching from 1 = 'do not agree at all' to 7 = 'fully agree'. The subscale Eeriness of the Uncanny Valley scale developed by Ho and MacDorman (2017) was implemented to determine the eeriness of the depicted virtual agent with eight items on a polarity 5-point scale: 'reassuring – eerie', 'numbing – freaky', 'ordinary – supernatural', 'unemotional – hair-rising', 'uninspiring - spine-tingling', boring -shocking', 'predictable – thrilling', 'bland – uncanny' and showed an acceptable internal consistency of α = .61. The open question 'What concerns would you have about sharing your personal data with AI in a context like the one shown in the video?' was also added for insights into the concerns regarding the transfer of personal data. Another open question was added, querying specifically about concerns regarding the usage of VR and an embodied AI for an exposure therapy session, i.e., 'What concerns would you have about conducting an exposure session in virtual reality with an embodied AI, as in the video shown?'.

3.1.5 Importance of different factors in AI and VR use for therapy

Participants were asked to rate the importance regarding different factors in the use of AI-directed therapy session on a 7-point Likert scale with the prefix 'It is important to me that…', reaching from 1 = 'not agree at all' to 7 = 'fully agree'. The factors were randomized and addressed a number of aspects, namely: '…the location of the AI's server is within Germany.', '…the location of the AI's server is within Europe.', '…I am aware about the company that developed the AI.', '…the AI was trained with data by real patients.', '…the location of development of the AI is within Europe.', '…my personal data is anonymized.', '…the use of the AI has been approved by the Ethic's Council.', '…the AI has been scientifically tested.', '…the AI has been tested within Europe.', '…another person is present during the session.', '…a therapist is present during the session.', '…I have control over the transfer of my personal data.', '…my data is only passed on within Europe.', '…the interaction with the AI is personalized to me.', '…I am aware which functions the AI has.', '…I am aware how the AI processes my data.', '…I have a good bond to the AI.', '…I am informed whether the virtual person is an AI and not a real person.' and '…the AI is embodied and does not just have a voice.'. The video showcased in the pre-study can be found in the electronic supplemental material. The importance of the different factors was measured on a 7-point Likert scale as it is shown to provide a more precise depiction of opinions (see Finstad, 2010). All the items were randomized.

3.2 Results Pre-Study

In the following the results for the pre-study are presented, including the descriptives and results regarding the questionnaire as well as a summary of the answers given for the implemented open questions. The results were calculated using IBM SPSS Statistics 29.0.2.0.

3.2.1 Affinity for Technology Interaction, Trust and Privacy Attitudes Questionnaire

The overall Mean and Standard Deviation of the Affinity for Technology Interaction (ATI) scale in this questionnaire for $N = 152$ was $M = 4.66$ and $SD = 1.18$. To determine participants' general trust disposition, the subscale propensity to trust was assessed, which consisted of three items. The overall Mean and Standard Deviation of the subscale were $M = 3.55$ and $SD = 1.47$. Furthermore, the participant's attitude towards Trust and Data Security were conducted with 17 items and showed a Mean and Standard Deviation for $N = 152$ participants of $M = 3.56$ and $SD = 1.19$. The attitudes of participants regarding privacy were conducted on 17 items, i.e., the two subscales interest in protection (P) and willingness to share personal information (PI) of the Privacy Attitude Questionnaire (PAQ). For the 152 participants, the overall Mean and Standard Deviation for the P scale were $M = 4.66$ and $SD = 0.91$, and $M = 2.95$ and $SD = 0.85$ for the PI subscale. Additionally, the perceived informedness about the use of AI in mental health care was assessed on one item and showed an overall Mean of $M = 3.57$ and $SD = 1.29$. All descriptives are visualized in Table 3.1.

Table 3.1 Scales of personal disposition measured on a 7-point Likert scale

Scale	*M*	*SD*
Affinity for Technology Interaction (ATI)	4.66	1.18
Propensity to Trust	3.55	1.47
Trust and Data Security	3.56	1.19
Interest in Protection (P)	4.66	0.91
Willingness to share Personal Information (PI)	2.95	0.85
Informedness AI in healthcare	3.57	1.29

3.2.2 Perception of and Attitudes towards the Virtual Agent, AI and Data Security

No participants had to be excluded due to failing the attention checks. The overall Mean and Standard Deviation of the participants' Attitudes regarding Security of Personal Data amounted to $M = 5.13$ and $SD = 0.72$ (see Table 3.2).

Table 3.2 Items of the Attitudes regarding Security of Personal Data on a 7-point Likert scale

Items	*M*	*SD*
The right to access health data is very important to me.	5.61	1.24
Data security is very important to me.	5.40	1.41
Improving emergency care is important to me.	5.84	1.14
I would be willing to disclose my personal data to improve emergency care, e.g., for research purposes. (recoded)	4.91	1.55
I am concerned about insufficient protection of my personal data.	4.91	1.57
I have no concerns about entrusting an AI with my sensitive data. (recoded)	2.97	1.61
I would feel more comfortable disclosing my data if I was accurately informed about the use of my sensitive data.	5.72	1.41
I would feel more comfortable disclosing my data if I could determine exactly which of my data is stored.	5.68	1.39

To assess the Attitudes towards AI Use in therapy, seven items were used. The items showed an overall Mean and Standard Deviation of $M = 3.36$ and $SD = 1.46$. The self-created items of the scale can be seen in Table 3.3.

Table 3.3 Items for measuring the Attitude towards AI and VR Use in therapy on a 7-point Likert scale

Items	*M*	*SD*
I would feel comfortable conducting a therapy session with an embodied AI as a therapist.	3.38	1.89
I would like to conduct an exposure therapy session in virtual reality.	4.02	1.92
I would feel comfortable entrusting my personal data to an AI during a therapy session.	3.27	1.76
I would be willing to disclose my sensitive data for research purposes in order to contribute to the improvement of AI.	3.98	1.89
I would trust an embodied AI as a therapist in the same way as a real therapist.	2.92	1.77
I believe that an AI could help me with my problems just as well as a real therapist.	3.06	1.72
I believe that over time I could build up a similar relationship with an AI as I would with a real therapist.	2.90	1.84

To assess the attitudes towards the depicted Virtual Agent, the Uncanny Valley subscale Eeriness was used, which showed an overall Mean and Standard Deviation of $M = 2.54$ and $SD = 0.51$ for 150 valid cases. Moreover, the preference of different therapy approaches compared to no therapy were measured on three different items for $N = 151$ participants with the highest values for a human therapist ($M = 6.71$, $SD = 0.81$), followed by an embodied AI accompanied by a human therapist ($M = 5.77$, $SD = 1.38$) and lowest values for an embodied AI ($M = 4.66$, $SD = 1.85$). The means were compared in a repeated-measures Anova, Mauchly's Test of Sphericity was significantly under $p < .05$, therefore, the Greenhouse-Geisser correction for degrees of freedom was used (Field, 2024), showing a significant difference in preference for therapy form, $F(1.49, 393.15) = 120.89$, $p < .001$, partial $\eta^2 = .45$.

Moreover, the participants were asked about the importance of different factors for the use of AI in therapy (see Table 3.4) for 150 valid participants.

Table 3.4 Level of importance regarding different factors measured on a 7-point Likert scale

Item	*M*	*SD*
The AI has been scientifically tested	6.30	1.14
Control over data disclosure	6.07	1.36
Being informed whether the virtual person is an AI and not a real person	5.97	1.39
Anonymization of personal data	5.93	1.38
Knowledge about how the AI processes data	5.87	1.35
Knowledge about the AI's functions	5.84	1.31
Interaction with the AI is customized to me	5.65	1.45
The AI was trained with data from real patients	5.64	1.28
The use of AI is supported by the Ethic's Council	5.35	1.58
Awareness which company has developed the AI	5.21	1.68
A therapist being present during the session	5.14	1.68
The AI has been tested within Europe	4.96	1.69
Location of the AI's server within Europe	4.69	1.86
A good relationship with the AI	4.61	1.70
Data only shared within Europe	4.58	1.88
Location of the AI's server within Germany	4.50	1.93
The AI being embodied and not just depicted through voice	4.39	1.87
Another person being present during the session	4.19	1.91
The development location of the AI is within Europe.	4.09	1.80

Note. The prefix of each item was 'It is important to me that…'.

A Multiple Linear Regression was conducted to examine the relationship between the predictors ATI, Trust Disposition, Trust and Data Security, PAQ subscale P, PAQ subscale PI and the dependent variable Attitude AI Use. The overall model was significant ($F(5, 144) = 13.66$, $p < .001$) and accounted for 32.2% of the variance in the Attitude towards AI Use ($R^2 = .322$, adjusted $R^2 = .298$). The multicollinearity between the predictors was acceptable with tolerance values between 0.797 and 0.987 and the highest variance inflation factor (VIF) well below 10 (1.25). Among the different predictors, higher Trust and Data Security values significantly predicted more positive Attitudes towards AI Use ($\beta = .475$, $t = 6.47$, $p < .001$), as well as higher willingness to disclose personal information (PI) ($\beta = .201$, $t = 2.61$, $p = .010$). The three predictors

ATI (β = .100, t = 1.39, p = .168), Trust Disposition (β = –.050, t = –.73, p = .468) and PAQ subscale P (β = .052, t = .69, p = .490) did not significantly predict Attitude towards AI Use.

A second Multiple Linear Regression tested the same five predictors on Attitudes regarding Security of Personal Data. The overall model was significant ($F(5, 145) = 7.12$, $p < .001$) and accounted for 19.7% variance in the Attitudes regarding Security of Personal Data ($R^2 = .197$, adjusted $R^2 = .169$). The subscale Interest in Protection (P) of the PAQ significantly predicted Attitudes regarding Security of Personal Data (β = .330, t = 4.01, $p < .001$), whereas the variables ATI (β = .084, t = 1.07, p = .285), Trust Disposition (β = .104, t = 1.38, p = .169), Trust and Data Security (β = .064, t = .81, p = .419) and subscale PI of the PAQ (β = –.158, t = –1.89, p = .061) were not significant predictors.

3.2.3 Open Questions regarding the concerns about data protection and AI use

Participants were asked about their concerns regarding the use of AI and VR for therapy in reference to the depicted video. The answers were summed up into clusters to facilitate ordering and comparing the concerns. The answer field for each question was unlimited, therefore, many participants discussed more than one issue. Thus, the total is made up of the sum of worries raised rather than the total number of participants. Each cluster is first defined shortly and then examples of comments are given. The following concerns regarding AI and VR use in mental health care have been discussed (see Figure 3.1), which naturally resulted in six clusters (number of people raising the issue):

➜ **Ineffectiveness of the Therapy, i.e., VR and AI therapy does not appear to** have the same effect as therapy with a human therapist for different reasons: (67)

- Looks unnatural
- Not immersive enough
- AI cannot relate/feel empathy like a human being
- Might feel misunderstood
- AI cannot read body language, facial expressions and interpret behaviour
- AI cannot mimic human closeness
- AI is limited in knowledge/actions

- Not enough support from AI (emotional support and create calming atmosphere)
- Inhumane look of agent might be distracting, elicit uncanny feeling
- Awareness that height is not real
- Does not look realistic enough
- Does not live up to human
- Might be too cautious and not ask uncomfortable questions, which might be necessary to identify certain problems or triggers
- Does not understand patient's feelings
- Effects not transferable to real life
- Not strong enough to trigger anxiety

➜ **Unsafe Intervention, i.e., the application appears to be unsafe for** different reasons: (48)

- AI cannot read body language, does not recognize sth. properly, underestimates feelings of users, user is crying
- AI has a bug—says sth. wrong/dangerous
- Training data set not of appropriate quality
- Patient fainting during session, Panic attack
- AI does not give enough support, causes harm
- Espionage
- No supervision of a real person in case of emergency
- Wrong interpretation of signals and words
- AI reacting to personal boundaries
- Wrong advice
- Wrong diagnosis
- AI might be rude and judgmental
- Losing touch with reality, misorientation
- Might not communicate real information (hallucinating or gaslighting)
- AI is not sufficiently qualified
- Technical difficulties

➜ **None, i. e., no concerns or interest/positive comments** (20)

➜ **Impersonal Treatment, i. e., the application elicits discomfort, or the embodied AI appears to be impersonal in its interaction:** (26)

- Unable to ask things
- Does not want AI to know fears
- Do not feel empathy for AI
- No bond
- Discomfort
- Trust towards AI

- Cannot open up
- Not personalized, does not cover personal needs
- Lack of human contact

➜ **Data Protection, i.e., concerns regarding the collection and transfer of** personal data shared within the therapy session: (16)

- Copying of data
- Data protection
- Transparency about which data is saved/used
- Things tracked/documented
- Third parties

➜ **Costs, i.e., concerns around the equipment:** (4)

- Expensive equipment
- Accessibility
- Quality of VR headset

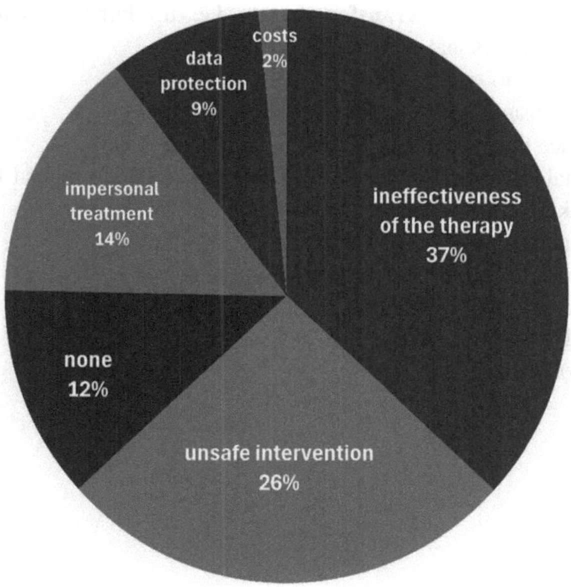

Fig. 3.1 Overview of the concerns regarding AI and VR use in mental health care

Additionally, the second open question queried participants about their concerns regarding the transfer of their data within the use of AI and VR for therapy (see Fig. 3.2). The following list summarizes the answers of the participants (number of times issue was raised):

➜ **Unauthorized Transfer of Data to Third Parties:** (68)
- Transferring to other doctors—anxiety disorder to urologist
- Unauthorized access of third parties—who sees data

➜ **Lack of Transparency, i.e., concerns regarding a lack of knowledge of** data processing: (66)
- Where does data go?—sold off for commercial purposes, etc.?
- How is the data processed?
- How long is data saved for?
- Used for training?
- Company handling AI—Inappropriate saving of data

➜ **Security Breaches:** (22)
- Server not protected enough
- Hacking

➜ **Discrimination due to Transfer of Data, i.e., the harm/consequences that** the transfer of personal data might lead to: (42)
- Transferred to employers
- Doctors/insurance could deny services
- Insurance could increase fee
- Potential employers might refuse employment due to mental health issues
- AI making wrong medical decisions
- Used against someone
- Traceable to identity of person (not anonymized)
- Sensitive data

➜ **General Discomfort** (6)

➜ **None** (25)

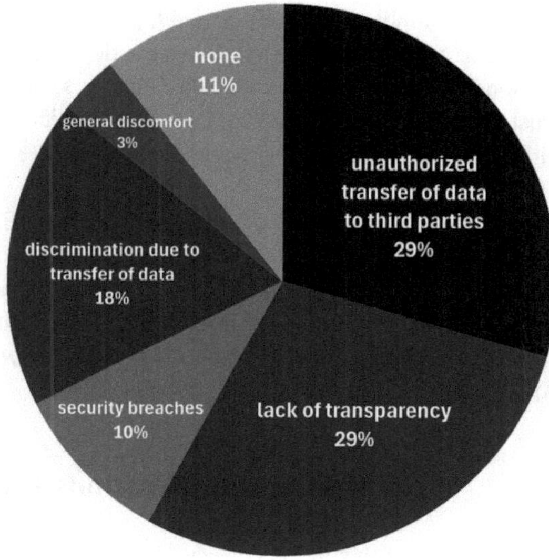

Fig. 3.2 Overview of the most frequent concerns regarding data disclosure in the context of AI and VR therapy summarized into clusters

3.2.4 Post-Hoc Calculations

A Pearson correlation between age and ATI shows a small non-significant negative correlation ($r = -.094$, $p = .251$, $N = 152$). A Linear Regression has been conducted to assess the relationship between ATI and the Attitude towards AI Use, which showed a significant correlation, $F(1, 149) = 4.32$, $p = .039$ and a variance explanation of $R^2 = .028$. To additionally assess the relationship between ATI and Attitude towards Security of Personal Data, a Linear Regression was conducted and resulted in higher values in ATI to significantly predict higher values in Attitude towards Security of Personal Data with an explained variance of $R^2 = .042$, $F(1, 149) = 6.52$, $p = .012$.

Moreover, the relationship between each of the two subscales from PAQ have been tested through a Linear Regression with the Attitude towards AI Use in mental health care, resulting in significant results for the PI subscale, $F(1, 148) = 12.73$, $p < .001$. The subscale PI showed an explained variance of $R^2 = .08$ with PI acting as a significant positive predictor for the Attitude towards AI Use, $B = 0.48$, $t(148) = 3.57$, $p < .001$. The subscale P showed a non-significant relationship with Attitudes towards AI Use, $F(1, 148) = 0.84$, $p = .361$.

Regarding the Trust and Data Security scale, a Linear Regression shows a non-significant relationship with the Attitude towards Security of Personal Data as a dependent variable, $F(1, 149) = 2.49$, $p = .117$. Additionally, a Linear Regression with Attitude towards AI Use as a dependent variable shows a significant relationship with the Trust and Data Security scale, $F(1, 148) = 58.18$, $p < .001$. Trust and Data Security acts as a positive predictor for Attitude towards AI Use with Trust and Data Security scale explaining 28% variance, $B = 0.65$, $t(148) = 7.63$, $p < .001$.

The effect of the level of informedness regarding AI use in health care is non- significant for the dependent variable Attitude towards Security of Personal Data, $F(1, 149) = 1.41$, $p = .237$ with informedness explaining a variance of $R^2 = .009$. The effect of informedness on Attitude towards AI Use shows a non-significant correlation $F(1, 148) = 3.35$, $p = .069$ with informedness explaining 0.22% of the attitude towards AI use.

3.3 Discussion and Implications for the Main Study

The pre-study of this thesis consists of an online questionnaire, querying patients about prevailing concerns of deploying AI and VR in mental health care with the example of a VRET for the treatment of acrophobia in the form of a video. The study design and the results of the questionnaire are discussed in the following sections.

3.3.1 Measures and Study Design

The prevalent study is an exploratory approach, thus various items were self-created and only partially based on validated questionnaires. Moreover, the chosen relevant factors and open questions put a particular focus on Data Security and whilst the questionnaire aims at covering the majority of possible issues, it remains biased due to prevailing literature findings. Therefore, certain concerns could have still gone undetected. Overall, the implemented scales, including the self-created items, e.g., Attitude towards AI Use showed relatively high internal consistency. For the PAQ the internal consistency was comparably low with $\alpha = .67$ and $\alpha = .66$. However, the original scale developed by Chignell et al. (2003) consisted of more subscales than the two used for the purpose of this study.

The questionnaire entails an example video, focusing on an exposure therapy treatment approach for acrophobia, i.e., fear of heights, defined as a form of anxiety disorder. Therefore, it is important to note that while the purpose of this work is to determine general concerns of patients in mental health care and implement resulting implications, the generalizability of the findings is limited. The depicted environment and quality of the virtual agent, which is still an earlier prototype of the application, might have additionally altered people's perception of AI and VR in mental health care.

Moreover, participants were only presented with a video and did not experience an immersive experience in VR (e.g., Rimer et al., 2021). Additionally, the video was relatively short and only showed a summary of the interaction, which may have suggested that the patient has very little control over the procedure of the session. The study also has not previously been approved by the Ethic's council of the university due to limited timing, however, in hindsight this could have ensured participants' well-being, which should be a priority when exploring AI in mental health care.

3.3.2 Most Important Factors

The ratings of the importance of different factors showed the following five factors to be rated as the most important when using AI and VR in therapy:

1. 'AI has been scientifically tested'
2. 'Control over data disclosure'
3. 'Being informed whether the virtual person is an AI and not a real person'
4. 'Anonymization of personal data'
5. 'Knowledge about how the AI processes data'

The order of the factors emphasizes the relevance of different aspects that might affect (future) users' attitude and trust towards the application and their experience during a VR therapy session with an embodied AI. However, it is important to note that only a handful of factors were listed in the overall rating. The five factors highest in rating specifically underline the importance of transparency (knowledge about communicating with an AI; knowledge about how data is being processed), and control and the security of their personal data. In comparison, location-specific information, e.g., where was the AI developed, is data saved on a server within Europe, etc. appears to be less relevant.

Furthermore, the scientific testing and approval is the most important factor, whereas the approval of the Ethic's Council results in a much lower rating. This reflects the assumptions made prior to this study, pointing out that although there are a variety of ethical guidelines that have been formulated (see Fiske et al.,

2019; Obremski & Wienrich, 2024), they might not entirely encompass patients' concerns or play an important role in their life.

3.3.3 Concerns regarding Data Security and AI Use

The two open questions allowed the participants to openly state their concerns about the general use of AI and VR, and the related data security by encouraging a less guided impression in comparison to the rating of fixed items. The open question field was unlimited in characters, therefore, many participants voiced different issues and concerns within their answers. The concerns about AI Use in mental health care showed the highest concern of potential users to be the inefficacy of VR and AI therapy. The therapy approach has been repeatedly compared to human therapists and the shortcomings AI and VR might have in comparison. The lower quality of the interaction and environment could have added to the concerns about the inefficacy of a therapy approach using VR and AI. Whereas the need for a comparable quality of treatment and involving mental health care professionals is addressed in the formulated ethical guidelines for AI in mental health care (Kuhn et al., 2009; Tavory, 2024), the risk of inefficacy does not come up as a stand-alone regulation. However, it could be argued that covering prevailing ethical principles and advancing developmental and research efforts contributes to the overall efficacy of the treatment. Although the effectiveness of VR in the treatment of anxiety disorders has been established through meta-analyses (Krijn et al., 2004; Morina et al., 2015), it should be further examined how these findings could be communicated to patients or presented in future applications. Impersonal treatment, i.e., the lack of a humane and personalized approach when interacting with embodied AI takes up the third most frequent concern, which underlines the importance of the bond between patient and therapist within a therapy session (Parish & Eagle, 2003). It also reflects the focus on HCAI in the development of AI-controlled applications in mental health care. The second highest concern is the possibility of an unsafe intervention, i.e., the concern that there are not enough safety mechanisms in place, particularly with no human being present during the session. Especially medical issues have been raised, for instance, how it would be handled if the patient had a panic attack or faints. This further supports important ethical implications to consider when developing VRET applications, i.e., Risk Avoidance principle (see Obremski & Wienrich, 2024).

The fourth largest concern was 'none' and shows a generally positive attitude towards VR and AI use for therapy. However, it is relevant to state that many participants mentioned that there are no concerns with the specific anxiety disorder depicted in the video, which may look different for other mental disorders. Data security poses the second smallest concern, which was possibly moderated by the second open question regarding concerns about data disclosure, which had already come up earlier within the questionnaire. On the other hand, it could be argued that privacy concerns could have been more frequently mentioned due to the priming of participants with this issue previously, which was not the case (Higgins et al., 1985).

The second open question was supposed to give further insight into the concerns when disclosing personal data during the use of AI and VR for therapy. The two most frequent worries are a lack of transparency, i.e., the concern that users are not informed how their data is processed and secondly, the unauthorized transfer to third parties. The first one expresses the general need for humans to act autonomously and possess control over their actions and identity as postulated in the Self-Determination Theory (Deci & Ryan, 2012). Whilst the second one is similar to a lack of transparency, it emphasizes the specifically voiced concerns regarding 'third parties', i.e., organizations that might use their data without their consent or knowledge.

The second largest worry is possible harm/discrimination, which includes the consequences that might arise from data disclosure, such as disadvantages at work or other places. This concern raises the relevance of previous findings, pointing out negative stereotypes and an overall negative stigma surrounding mental illness (Corrigan & Rüsch, 2002). It emphasizes participants' need for a thorough anonymization of their data and a high level of autonomy and transparency. However, it should be noted here, too, that many participants did not see any issues with disclosing their data. The nature of the depicted anxiety disorder was mentioned as well, as it is not seen as a mental illness that requires the disclosure of compromising personal information.

3.3.4 Further Calculations

The results on the preferences of therapy type between human therapist, embodied AI, and embodied AI accompanied by a human therapist show the human therapist alone to be the most preferred type of therapy with an embodied AI alone being rated the lowest. All the therapy types were put in comparison to no therapy, therefore, whilst embodied AI alone was rated the lowest it is still preferred over no therapy. The factor of another person being present during the session seems to be the second least important factor. Putting these two results together, patients appear to not actively be concerned by the intervention itself and to be left alone, however, emphasize the importance of involvement of professionals and their expertise. The EU AI Act accompanies this as well with Human Oversight discussed in Article 14 (European Parliament, 2024).

The overall informedness about the use of AI in (mental) health care was relatively low, which raises the question about *AI literacy* within society, i.e., the ability to effectively and appropriately interact with AI (Long & Magerko, 2020). Despite the growing distribution of AI in everyday technology, such as smartphones, smart speakers, etc., the handling of AI is not necessarily taught in school or universities unless it is relevant to the field of study. In turn, this might contribute to the observed low values regarding the attitudes towards AI and VR use in therapy. Phenomena like the *Mere Exposure Effect* suggest an increase in positive attitudes towards something when repeatedly interacting with it (Bornstein, 1989). Future research might benefit from measuring AI literacy and exploring the effect it has on other factors and vice versa. Especially the bond between patient and therapist has come up as a relevant aspect in comparison with AI and its importance for the effectiveness of exposure therapy should be further examined. Furthermore, results show a relatively low level of perceived eeriness, suggesting that the depicted agent did not elicit high levels of eeriness or discomfort in the participants. This supports previous work on improving the agent's realism.

Furthermore, the willingness to disclose personal information (PI) and high Trust and Data Security values significantly predict more positive Attitudes towards AI Use.

This to an extent reflects the understanding that interacting with AI inevitably results in the need to disclose data as individuals with higher willingness to share information or higher trust exhibit more positive attitudes towards AI use in mental health care. In turn, it suggests that participants less willing to share their data show more negative attitudes towards AI use in mental health care, insinuating that the perceived data security can alter the attitude towards the application as a whole. The explained variance of the Multiple Linear Regression conducted with the dependent variable Attitudes towards AI Use was below 40% with the chosen five predictors, therefore, a further analysis of predictors for the Attitudes towards AI Use might be necessary.

3.3.5 Summary and Implications Main Study

The most important concerns were the fear of inefficacy and unsafe intervention for general AI and VR use. The specific concerns surrounding data security appeared to be the lack of transparency and the unauthorized transfer to third parties. The five factors highest rated in importance are: 'AI has been scientifically tested', 'Control over data disclosure', 'Being informed whether the virtual person is an AI and not a real person', 'Anonymization of personal data' and 'Knowledge about how the AI processes data'. While these findings reflect prevailing ethical guidelines, an additional principle came up through the exploratory approach of this pre-study, namely personalization of treatment.

Although inefficacy of treatment is one of the biggest concerns, it is not a tangible concept that can be manipulated, however, it is an iterative process that needs to be covered within ongoing research. Moreover, the importance of data security as a concern and as a predictor for the attitude about AI in mental health care has been underlined further through this work. Therefore, the main study addresses relevant topics surrounding this, namely transparency and autonomy, which appear as ethical guidelines and additionally aim at providing a more personalized interaction.

4 Main Study

The following section describes the main study, including the implementation of the application, measures, results and a discussion thereof.

4.1 Implementation

The application was developed using the Unity Engine version 2022.3.23f1. The following section describes the implementation of the application, which has already been displayed in the video used in the pre-study at an earlier stage.

4.1.1 Virtual Environment

The project described in Obremski and Wienrich (2024) was developed further, and the same environment was used as discussed in their work. The current study is supposed to pave the way for safe future applications for the treatment of mental health disorders, using VR and AI, e.g., in the form of exposure therapy. However, as the risks of exposing participants to possibly harmful stimuli remain, this study lets users partake in an initial therapeutic conversation rather than conducting a complete exposure session. The participants are transported to

Supplementary Information The online version contains supplementary material available at https://doi.org/10.1007/978-3-658-50067-2_4.

P. Friedrich, *To be healed or to be hacked*, BestMasters,
https://doi.org/10.1007/978-3-658-50067-2_4

a terrace after the conversation, to assess the feeling of safety for future development. Therefore, people suffering from fear of heights were excluded from the study. The setting of the virtual environment is supposed to resemble the initial contact with a psychotherapist, thus, the virtual agent and the user are positioned opposite each other at an office table (see Fig. 4.1), allowing a more formal character compared to a setting, where both parties sit on a couch. On top of the table are objects commonly found in an office, i.e., a coffee mug, a notebook, pens, books. There is a picture with a bright landscape attached to the wall behind the virtual agent. To the right of the user is a street with cars continuously passing by the window. The lighting of the scene consists of one directional light outside the window with soft shadows and a temperature mode of 6285, giving a warm yellow tint to the scene. The directional light is baked rather than real-time to enhance performance. An additional spotlight source is attached to the desk lamp, which is directed towards the virtual agent (see left corner in Fig. 4.1). To increase the user's immersion, additional audio sources were added to the respective objects, such as a car. Additionally, the reverb zone 'room' was assigned to the office room prefab, resulting in the distorting of audio and adjustment of volume from sounds coming from outside the room (Unity Technologies, 2024).

Fig. 4.1 The virtual environment showing the setting of the virtual agent opposite from the user

The entire dialogue with the embodied AI happens within this setting. The user is transported to a terrace after the end of the interaction and is free to look around there (see Fig. 4.2).

Fig. 4.2 The virtual environment showing the final scene on the terrace of the building

4.1.2 VR Questionnaires –MC and Self-Disclosure

The participants' self-disclosure is measured using a questionnaire within the VR environment as self-disclosure during the interaction with the embodied AI would have been more difficult to evaluate. Furthermore, more data, i.e., audio recordings of the participants' dialogue with the embodied AI would have been needed to effectively assess the hypotheses, potentially interfering with the actual manipulation. The questionnaires are all 2D in world space and appear at the respective points of the interaction next to the embodied AI, thus both the AI and the questionnaire are in the Field of View (FOV) of the participant simultaneously. A 2D layout has previously shown to be easier to use and preferred over a 3D questionnaire (Safikhani et al., 2021). Additionally, the VR questionnaires are supposed to disrupt the interaction as little as possible and for the participant to remain in their place, where they can still see the embodied AI. This might be aggravated when implementing a 3D questionnaire, which requires participants to get up and touch virtual buttons.

When designing virtual UI elements, many aspects must be considered to maintain the immersion and usability of the virtual environment and the interactable object itself. Accordingly, the contrast ratio of the colour of the panel and the instructions and statements is kept relatively high (black, dark red and dark blue on white) to facilitate readability and maintain user experience (Gabbard et al., 1999). The current accessibility guidelines recommend a minimum ratio of 4.5:1 for normal text and suggest higher values for smaller displays (Caldwell et al., 2008). The human viewing angle both horizontally and vertically for comfortable reading in HMD is limited to around 30° from the center, i.e., a total of 60° (Jerald, 2015), which has been considered for the size and position of the questionnaire canvas relative to the participant. The panel's alpha value is set to 100 (out of 255). This mid-level transparency allows the environment behind the panel to remain slightly visible, which helps preserve immersion by blending the UI element with the virtual environment (see Fig. 4.3). For the selection of elements on the canvas a raycast is used. The canvas is placed far enough to lie entirely within the user's FOV, yet close enough to minimize arm fatigue from holding up the controller in mid-air (Bowman et al., 2001). A visual of the controller is also added and remains visible, while the raycast beam is only rendered when the VR questionnaires are active. The scale points are selected through toggles controlled by Unity's Toggle Group component, ensuring single-choice answers, e.g., out of seven toggles only one can be selected at a time. Providing immediate feedback on the user's actions has been shown to enhance user experience and reduce errors (Nielsen & Molich, 1990). Therefore, hover highlights, i.e., when moving the point of the raycast over a toggle it changes color to a darker grey, and sound cues on selection were incorporated.

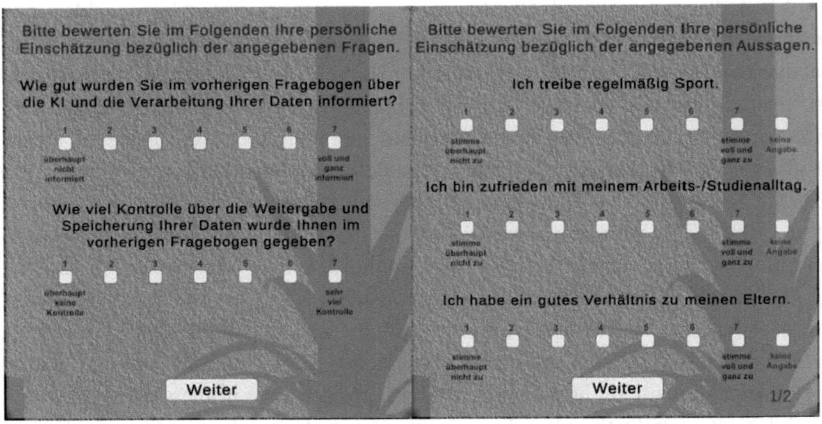

Fig. 4.3 The VR questionnaires for the manipulation check (left) and the first set of sensitive questions (right)

The questionnaire commences with two manipulation checks, which assess the manipulation regarding transparency and autonomy in the previously presented computer- based questionnaire. The manipulation of transparency and autonomy was assessed through the following two questions: 'How well were you informed about AI and the processing of your data in the previous questionnaire?' and 'How much control over the transfer and collection of your data was given to you in the previous questionnaire?', which were to be answered on a 7-point Likert scale reaching from 'not at all informed/no control' to 'fully informed/a lot of control' (see Fig. 4.3). To determine the amount of self-disclosure carried out within an interaction with an embodied AI in VR, the questionnaires cover different topics. The first set of sensitive questions covers less sensitive topics, including sports, satisfaction with work/studying, and the relationship with one's parents (see Fig. 4.3). Participants were asked to indicate how much they agree with each statement on a 7-point Likert scale from 1 = 'do not agree at all' to 7 = 'fully agree' with the possibility to select 'no indication'. The first set of questions to indicate the amount of self-disclosure was put before the more intimate questions, following the idea of the foot-in-the-door paradigm, which suggests that asking for a smaller favour first increases willingness for people to grant a bigger favour later (Freedman et al., 1966; Guéguen, 2002).

Disclosing sensitive, even shameful information about oneself is crucial in psychotherapy. The willingness to share more sensitive or compromising information, which are oftentimes topics that are barely discussed or even lied about, i.e., sexual behaviour, substance abuse and violent thoughts are assessed on a second panel (Blanchard & Farber, 2016; Farber & Hall, 2002; Weiner & Shuman, 1984). The three statements are to be rated on a 7-point Likert scale from 1 = 'do not agree at all' to 7 = 'fully agree' with the possibility to select 'no indication' (see Fig. 4.4).

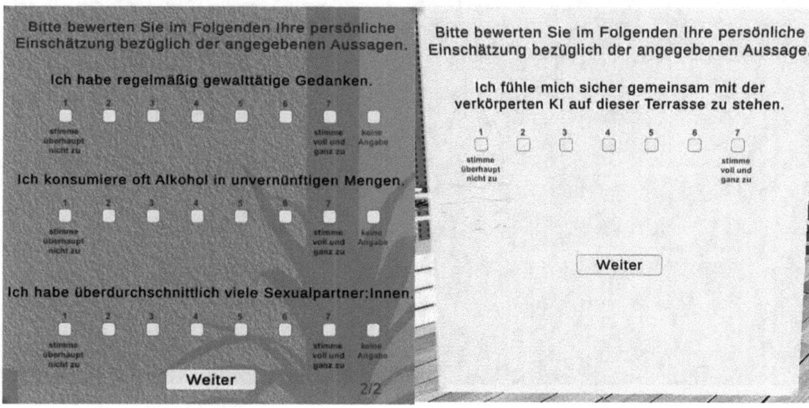

Fig. 4.4 The VR Questionnaires for the second set of sensitive questions (left) and the safety check on the terrace (right)

To save the answer of each statement the Question_Saving.cs script has been created, which entails a method that iterates over each toggle group within the panels previously assigned in the inspector and extracts the numerical value of the name of the currently active toggle, e.g., 'Agr1', 'Agr7' or assigns the default value '−9' if no answer has been selected (see Fig. 4.5).

```
public void SaveAnswer(GameObject panel, string topic)
{

    // find the toggle groups within the panel
    ToggleGroup[] toggleGroups = panel.GetComponentsInChildren<ToggleGroup>();
    Debug.Log($"Saving answers for {topic}, found {toggleGroups.Length} toggle groups.");

    foreach (ToggleGroup toggleGroup in toggleGroups)
    {
        // name from parent object
        string questionName = toggleGroup.gameObject.name;

        // find toggle
        Toggle activeToggle = toggleGroup.GetComponentsInChildren<Toggle>().FirstOrDefault(toggle => toggle.isOn);

        // creation of answer string taken from digit in toggle object name
        string answer =
            activeToggle ? new string(activeToggle.gameObject.name.Where(char.IsDigit).ToArray()) : "-9";

        if (answers.ContainsKey(questionName))
        {
            answers[questionName] = answer;
        }
        else
        {
            answers.Add(questionName, answer);
        }

        Debug.Log($"Saved answer for {questionName}: {answer}");
    }
}
```

Fig. 4.5 A screenshot of the code extracting the answers from the ToggleGroup

Each answer is first saved in a dictionary and eventually stored in a csv file, where the participant's ID and the timestamp of when the answers are collected is appended. Each 'Continue' button has an OnClick event, triggering the SaveAnswer() function for all answers on the respective panel. To ensure each answer has been properly saved, a delayed coroutine is implemented. The order of the answers is defined in an array within the SaveFinalData() function, which is called with the 'Continue' button on the last panel (see Fig. 4.6).

```
public void SaveFinalData()
{
    // local copy of current answers
    Dictionary<string, string> finalAnswers = new Dictionary<string, string>(answers);

    // create a timestamp
    string timeStamp = System.DateTime.Now.ToString(("dd/MM/yyyy HH:mm:ss tt zz"));

    // list of expected questions in order
    string[] expectedQuestions = new string[]
    {
        "MC_Transparenz",
        "MC_Autonomie",
        "Sport",
        "Arbeit",
        "Eltern",
        "Agression",
        "Alkohol",
        "Sexualverhalten",
        "Safety AI"
    };

    // build csv line
    System.Text.StringBuilder csvLine = new System.Text.StringBuilder();
    csvLine.Append(participantID);
    csvLine.Append(",");
```

Fig. 4.6 A code screenshot showing the dictionary for the saving logic of the VR questionnaire answers

Additionally, with the final 'Continue' button all toggles are reset, thus allowing for each new participant to select the toggles on the VR questionnaire anew (see Fig. 4.7).

```
// resetting all toggles to be unticked
public void ResetAllToggles()
{
    ToggleGroup[] toggleGroups = FindObjectsOfType<ToggleGroup>(true);
    Debug.Log("Found Toggle Groups: " + toggleGroups.Length);

    foreach (ToggleGroup group in toggleGroups)
    {
        // loop through toggles in group and uncheck them
        foreach (Toggle toggle in group.GetComponentsInChildren<Toggle>())
        {
            toggle.SetIsOnWithoutNotify(false);
        }
    }

    Debug.Log("All toggles unticked!");
}
```

Fig. 4.7 A code screenshot of resetting all the toggles

4.1.3 Virtual Agent

The virtual agent was designed in a way to resemble a female therapist in her mid-30s, wearing a beige long-sleeve turtleneck with dark jeans (see Fig. 4.1). The agent was designed with the Reallusion Character Creator 4 and various animations, e.g., sitting_listening and facial expressions, e.g., big_smile, compassionate. Facial features were kept soft, and eyes and hair are both a light brown color. In the Unity Engine, the virtual agent's shaders for respective body parts were adjusted, e.g., for the eyes the Avatar/EyeShapeShader and Avatar/AvatarShader for the skin. To increase the virtual agent's realism, not just visually, but also behaviorally (Groom et al., 2009), various animations and facial expressions are triggered at random within a set interval. Two additional layers were created in the Animator Controller, namely 'facial_expressions' and 'gestures', which each have an AnimatorMask attached. For the facial expressions everything is excluded but the head, whereas the arm gestures layer has a mask attached, excluding anything but head, left and right arm. This allows a more precise control of the virtual agent's movement. Non-verbal behavior aids understanding, while also making virtual agents appear higher in warmth and competence and fostering interpersonal empathy (Biancardi et al., 2017; Wang & Ruiz, 2021). Appropriate non-verbal behavior should align with the content of speech (Delbosc et al., 2023), therefore, to fit the general course of the conversation as speech is generated in real-time and animations cannot be timed to the content of the speech, animations are separated in listening (isSalsaing) and talking (!isSalsaing), controlled through the SALSA Lip-Sync plugin from Crazy Minnow Studios (see Fig. 4.8).

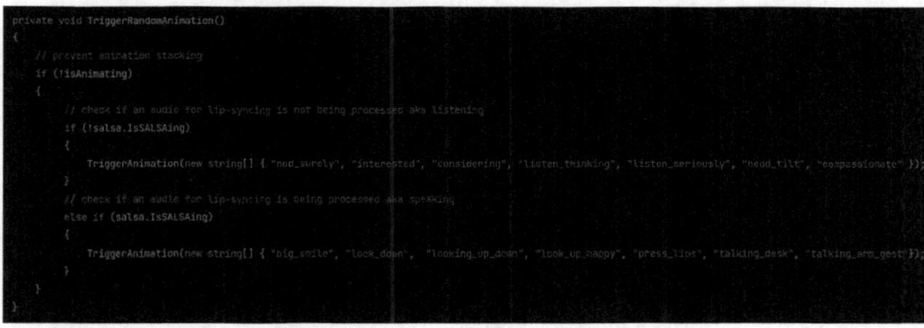

Fig. 4.8 A screenshot of the code triggering animations when the agent is listening or speaking

Additionally, a cooldown of animations has been added to ensure animations do not overlap and cause breaks in realistic behaviors (see Fig. 4.9).

```
private void TriggerAnimation(string[] animationTriggers)
{
    // preventing triggering of animation mid-gesture
    if (isAnimating) return;

    // Ensure the animator is not null before proceeding
    if (animationTriggers.Length == 0)
    {
        Debug.LogWarning("No animation states.");
        return;
    }

    // randomly pick animation from array
    string selectedAnimation = animationTriggers[Random.Range(0, animationTriggers.Length)];

    // set the chosen animation parameter to true
    animator.SetTrigger(selectedAnimation);

    Debug.Log($"Triggered animation: {selectedAnimation}");

    // start cooldown for animations
    StartCoroutine(AnimationCooldown(Random.Range(2f, 4f)));
}
```

Fig. 4.9 A screenshot of the code adding a cooldown for the agent's animations

Measures taken in pursuit of increasing the virtual agent's realism, apart from adjusting features and clothing in the CC4 program, also included tuning of viseme easings, i.e., the visual movements of mouth and face for the different phonemes in the spoken language controlled by SALSA Lip-Sync. A LookTarget, i.e., a child object of the XR Origin has been assigned to control the gaze direction of the virtual agent as gaze plays an important role for interpersonal non-verbal communication (Cook, 1977). The focus of the virtual agent's gaze is thus on the user, however, to appear more natural and not be fixed on the user continuously, the Affinity of the LookTarget is set to 0.86%, resulting in the virtual agent looking around the room occasionally. Apart from the random animations and facial expressions imported from the Reallusion Character Creator, the EmoteR is utilized for triggering random expressions, e.g., 'soften', which entails mouth smile left and right, and brow raise of inner brow left and right, as well as eye squint left and right. The general idle movement for every scene wherein the virtual agent is positioned at the desk in the therapy room is a sitting animation with the virtual agent's hands placed on the knees. The sixth scene on the terrace triggers the standing idle animation through setting the layer weight of the sitting layer to 0 and the standing layer to 1.

4.1.4 Interaction—GPT, Text-to-Speech and Prompt Sheet

The virtual agent is connected to the platform OpenAI, widely known as the developers of the AI Chatbot Generative Pre-trained Transformer (ChatGPT). The API to OpenAI allows communication with one of their most recent models (March 2025) GPT4o in the realm of this study. Within the OpenAI Playground an assistant can be created, and the API key thereof is then passed in a script in the Unity project. The real-time communication between the user and the embodied AI entails various steps: The user is instructed to press 'A' on the right controller when immersed in the VR environment, then the user's speech is transcribed, i.e., Speech-to-Text through using Microsoft Azure. The text is then sent to the GPT4o assistant, which generates the respective response through synthetic speech using the Text-to-Speech platform ElevenLabs. The embodied AI in this study utilizes the professional voice 'Leonie' provided by the ElevenLabs available voices. The prefab of the virtual agent consequently has the following scripts assigned: TTS Azure (Speech-to-Text), TTS Open AI (GPT4o API) and TTS Eleven Labs (Text-to-Speech). Considering the process of the audio generation, it can lead to latency when interacting with the embodied AI, therefore, a loading bar has been added, to indicate feedback regarding the status of the audio generation and facilitate mutual understanding. The set up of this pipeline was done by another student and is consequently not explained in more detail in this work.

The GTP4o model was previously prompted with an extensive description on how to conduct the therapy session, i.e., the Prompt Sheet, presented in detail in the electronic supplemental material. The temperature of the AI assistant was set to 0.9 in the OpenAI playground. Higher temperature values lead to a more creative output (Murel & Nobel, 2024). The Prompt Sheet entails the entire procedure of the interaction in VR and controls the transition of scenes and activation of the respective VR Questionnaire panels handled in the PlayerController.cs script. The aim of the interaction is for the participant to briefly get to know the embodied AI and gain insight into relevant practices for exposure therapy, e.g., breathing techniques. The interaction does not directly address mental health issues of the participant or entails a lengthy dialogue for several reasons. The research regarding embodied AI and VR for a therapeutic intervention is still in its infancy, therefore, various factors should be examined first before the application is used in this context, specifically on 90 individuals, i.e., intended number of participants. Moreover, as the main manipulation consists of the amount of transparency and autonomy provided before the interaction and the self-disclosure is measured through the VR Questionnaire after the interaction, the effect of the interaction on self-disclosure is meant to be kept to a minimum. Through not discussing mental health issues or intending to diagnose it is easier to recruit a wider participant pool, which in turn allows a more diverse sample. Questions designed for the suspicion of anxiety disorders in a therapy session, e.g., 'Do you have sudden seizures that cause you to become frightened and suffer from symptoms such as a racing heart, trembling, sweating, shortness of breath, fear of death, etc.?' (Bandelow et al., 2015, p. 10) could trigger participants who may have been unaware about suffering from anxiety prior to the intervention and as the study does not provide follow-up mental health support, approaching a diagnosis is circumvented. The behavioral-therapy typical analysis of behavior, e.g., through the S-O-R-K-C model is thus also not utilized (Abbruzzese & Kübler, 2013).

The implemented instructions in the Prompt Sheet entail a general check of the participant's physical and psychological status, and low-level psychoeducation, which are overarching components of therapy approaches (Bandelow et al., 2015). After the embodied AI has introduced herself and checked with the participants whether their headset is properly put on, the embodied AI explains possible risks of VR usage. The check of the participant's physical state entails quality of sleep, caffeine and nicotine intake, medication intake, sickness and intake of sedatives prior to the interaction. Psychoeducation is provided through explaining a breathing and 'thinking-stop' technique and describing a stress scale from 0 to 100. Lastly, the embodied AI gives additional information about herself, i.e., she has studied psychology, has been a practicing psychotherapist for many years and her main area of expertise are anxiety disorders. The participant continuously is given the opportunity to ask questions, and the AI is instructed to await agreement of the participant at various stages of the interaction. The end of the sheet entails guidelines to appropriate behavior, the stress scale and the description of each scene in the virtual environment (see electronic supplemental material).

4.1.5 Transparency Manipulation

The information regarding data collection and the embodied AI differs among the three conditions. The relevant guidelines regulating data collection and AI use, i.e., General Data Protection Regulation (European Parliament, 2016) and the EU AI Act (European Parliament, 2024), however, determine a certain level of information and autonomy that needs to be given in this context. Therefore, for the control condition or 'legal condition', it is not feasible to provide no information or autonomy at all, thus the legal condition (1) provides minimal information and choices to cover the legally required regulations. The information (in condition (1) and (2)) must entail that the users are interacting with an AI-based system, the labelling of AI-generated material (European Parliament, 2024, Art. 50), and allow for the ability to put the AI-generated output into a context (European Parliament, 2024, Art. 13). Additionally, a GDPR form is provided prior to the participation of the study. Moreover, the participants are informed that the experimenter is always close by, following the Human Oversight discussed in Article 14 of the EU AI Act (European Parliament, 2024). Consequently, the information provided in the legal (1) and autonomy (2) condition, therefore, is presented before the interaction in VR within the questionnaire as such (see Fig. 4.10).

Informationen über die Interaktion mit der Künstlichen Intelligenz

Wer wird mir in VR gegenübersitzen?

- Im Folgenden werden Sie mit einer **verkörperten Künstlichen Intelligenz** interagieren.

Woher kommt die Stimme der Künstlichen Intelligenz?

- Alle Audioausgaben wurden **künstlich** generiert.

Hat die Künstliche Intelligenz einen vorgefertigten Text?

- Die Künstliche Intelligenz wurde zuvor mit Anweisungen ausgestattet, welche der Künstlichen Intelligenz dabei helfen entsprechend zu reagieren.

Fig. 4.10 A screenshot of the information provided in the legal condition questionnaire

The results from the pre-study showed 'lack of transparency' to be one of the biggest general concerns. Moreover, the concerns of 'unsafe intervention' and 'security breaches' as well as 'unauthorized transfer of data to third parties' and 'discrimination due to transfer of data' are accommodated in the transparency (3) condition. The statements 'being informed whether the virtual person is an AI and not a real person', 'knowledge about how the AI processes data' and 'knowledge about the AI's functions' were also among the ten highest rated important factors in the pre-study. Therefore, the following information is added in the computer-based questionnaire before the interaction in VR (see Fig. 4.11).

Informationen über die Interaktion mit der Künstlichen Intelligenz

Wer wird mir in VR gegenübersitzen?

- Im Folgenden werden Sie mit einer **verkörperten Künstlichen Intelligenz** interagieren.
- Eine Künstliche Intelligenz soll das **menschliche Denken** imitieren, indem diese mit großen Mengen an Daten trainiert wird und somit Informationen aufrufen kann.
- Es kann immer zu Fehlfunktionen kommen, jedoch wurden in dieser Studie **Vorkehrungen getroffen**, um dies so weit wie möglich zu verhindern.
- Im Rahmen dieser Studie wird das **neueste Modell von OpenAI** (ChatGpt 4o) verwendet.

Woher kommt die Stimme der Künstlichen Intelligenz?

- Alle Audioausgaben werden in Echtzeit **künstlich** von der Software ElevenLabs **generiert**, welche Text in Sprache umwandelt.

Hat die Künstliche Intelligenz einen vorgefertigten Text?

- Die Künstliche Intelligenz wurde zuvor mit einem ausführlichen **Info- und Anweisungsblatt** ausgestattet, welches der KI dabei helfen soll, entsprechend zu reagieren.
- Dieses Blatt enthält Anweisungen zum Ablauf der Sitzung, sowie **wichtige Informationen**, die von einer Therapeutin validiert wurden, wie beispielsweise relevante Atemtechniken.

Wie werden meine Daten verarbeitet?

- Die **allgemeinen** (nicht inhaltlichen) **Informationen** bei einer Nutzung von ChatGPT werden normalerweise analysiert, damit OpenAI nachvollziehen kann, wofür ihre Produkte verwendet werden.
- OpenAI speichert Daten von der Interaktion **bis zu 30 Tage** und löscht diese dann von ihrem System. Aufgrund von der Nutzung eines universitären Kontos im Rahmen dieser Studie werden gesammelte Daten **nicht für das Training** späterer Modelle von ChatGPT verwendet.
- Ihre Daten während der Interaktion mit der Künstlichen Intelligenz werden **anonymisiert** und unabhängig von den Daten ihres Fragebogens verarbeitet.

Wie werden meine Daten geschützt?

- Zusätzlich schützt OpenAI ihre Daten „at rest" durch eine **256-Bit Verschlüsselung**, d.h. alle Kombinationen auszuprobieren würde circa 1000 Jahre dauern.
- Daten, die im Umlauf sind, werden ebenfalls nach dem **industriellen Standard** für Datensicherheit verschlüsselt.
- Um Sicherheitsrisikos schnellstmöglich zu entdecken, gibt es ein **Sicherheitsteam**, welches 24/7/365 zur Verfügung steht.

Fig. 4.11 A screenshot of the information provided in the transparency condition questionnaire

The Cognitive Load Theory (Sweller, 2011) addresses the processing of information and emphasizes the concise display thereof to lower cognitive load. Rossi and Lenzini (2020) describe transparency-enhancing design as particularly the display of e.g., data collection guidelines entail many different aspects. These implications have been considered for the display of information of the transparency (3) condition. Specifically, the user-centric transparency has been put at the focus of design, and the information is described in a way which requires little prior knowledge about the topic. Based on the theory of chunking of information (see Miller, 1956), the text is separated into topics all starting with 'informative headings in the form of questions' (Rossi & Lenzini, 2020, p. 14). To ensure participants properly read through everything, there is a one-minute delay before the 'Continue' button for the questionnaire appears. The manipulation of Transparency and Autonomy within the questionnaire can be found in the electronic supplemental material. The increased transparency does not entail extensive amounts of information, to determine whether covering the concerns mentioned in the pre-study already suffices.

4.1.6 Autonomy Manipulation

The guidelines of the GDPR are met through the information provided in the GDPR form presented before the questionnaire and the creation of a personalized codeword, which allows the anonymous deletion of participants' data in the legal (1) and transparency (3) condition (European Parliament, 2016). The active choice herein entails a simple question regarding the data collection at the beginning of the questionnaire, i.e., 'Do you agree to your data being stored and would you like to continue participating in this study?' and the choices between 'Yes.' or 'No.'. If participants disagreed with the collection of their data, the final page of the questionnaire was called. The 'control over data disclosure' was the second highest rated important factor within the pre-study, therefore, the main study manipulates the control provided over data collection. Moreover, the concerns of 'unauthorized transfer of data to third parties' and 'discrimination due to transfer of data' are accommodated in the autonomy (2) condition through further data autonomy. Based on areas that might be of relevance when deploying AI and VR as part of a psychotherapeutic treatment, e.g., transfer of treatment status among medical professionals, etc. and the type of personal information shared during the demographic questions, the following additional questions were added before the VR interaction: 'Do you consent to your name being passed on to the Artificial Intelligence?', 'Do you consent to your age being passed on to the Artificial Intelligence?', 'Do you consent to your gender being passed on to the Artificial Intelligence?', 'Do you agree to share your previous experience of fear of heights with the Artificial Intelligence in order to personalize your therapy session to your previous experience?', 'Would you like the participation and content of this VR therapy session to be noted in your patient file?' (see in the electronic supplemental material). Each question had the options of 'Yes, I agree.' or 'No, I do not agree.'.

4.2 Measures

The following section provides the descriptives regarding the sample of the main study as well as the procedure and the measures used within the questionnaire. Each item that was recoded is marked with (R) respectively. The study was approved by the University's Ethic's Council.

4.2.1 Study Design and Participants

The study design consists of a three-way factorial between-subject design. The participants for this in-person experiment were randomly assigned to one of the three conditions: legal condition (1), autonomy condition (2), and transparency condition (3). The study was conducted on a Windows workstation (13th Gen Intel(R) Core(TM) i9- 13900 K, 64 GB RAM) with a Meta Quest Pro Head-Mounted Display (HMD) and the application was running on the 2022.3.23f1 Unity version. The study was conducted in person at a university building between the 19th of March and the 15th of May. Participants were able to decide between receiving the minimum wage per hour (12,82€ at the time of the study) or students in the Bachelor's courses media communications and HCI were able to receive one course credit in HCI or PIIS. The duration of the study was around 60 minutes. The participants were between 19 and 65 years old (M = 25.46, SD = 8.46). Of the N = 90 participants n = 67 (74.4%) were female and n = 23 (25.6%) identified as male. Participants indicated a variety of different education levels, namely n = 2 (2.2%) had a qualification for Mittlere Reife (Intermediate school leaving certificate), n = 61 (67.8%) Allgemeine Hochschulreife/Abitur (A-levels), n = 2 (2.2%) Fachabitur (Technical baccalaureate), n = 2 (2.2%) finished their apprenticeship, n = 18 (20.0%) have a Bachelor's degree and n = 5 (5.6%).

4.2.2 Procedure of the Study

On arrival participants were greeted and informed about the general procedure of the study. The study consisted of the first part of the questionnaire, interacting with an embodied AI in VR and then fulfilling the second part of the questionnaire. Participants were informed right away that there were going to be sensitive questions queried during the interaction with the embodied AI during which the experimenter is not present, yet close by in case any issues occur. The documents the participants were given included the creation of a codeword, extensive participant information on the participation, the GDPR and a written consent form. After signing the consent form, participants started with the first part of the questionnaire, which included a short introduction and agreement of participation, demographic data, and previous experiences with acrophobia. Depending on the condition, general information about the interaction was presented (1), and additional choices regarding data collection and processing were given (2) as well as additional, more extensive information about the embodied AI, the interaction and the data collection (3). After explaining the functionalities in VR and starting the Unity application, the experimenter left the room for the interaction in VR, which took around 15 minutes, regardless of the condition.

The participants sit on a chair at a desk like the set up in VR. Within VR, participants are instructed to first fill out the Manipulation Check panel and then start the conversation with the embodied AI by pressing the 'A' button on their controller. Once the embodied AI has been greeted, it follows the procedure set in the prompt sheet. Following the interaction, the embodied AI checks with the participant whether they have any questions and then transitions to the two panels, containing the sensitive questions. The participants are instructed to let the embodied AI know once they are finished and are then transported to the terrace with the embodied AI to fill out the final questionnaire. Finally, participants are instructed to take off the headset and let the experimenter know that the interaction is over. The final part of the computer-based questionnaire entails scales regarding trust towards the AI, previous use, perception of the AI (Godspeed, Uncanny Valley, PANAS) and self-created items regarding the participants' self-disclosure during the study. Finally, participants are thanked for their contribution and debriefed on the purpose of the study and the manipulation of autonomy and transparency.

4.2.3 Demographics

The demographic data that was collected consists of age, gender ('female', 'male', 'diverse', 'others'), and education ('no school-leaving certificate', 'secondary school leaving certificate', 'intermediate school-leaving certificate', 'general higher education entrance qualification/Abitur', 'university entrance qualification', 'completed vocational training', 'Bachelor's degree', 'Master's degree', 'doctorate'). Additionally, participants were instructed to think of previous experiences with heights and rate the three self-created items on a 7-point Likert scale from 1 = 'do not agree at all' to 7 = 'totally agree': 'I have no problem with height.' (R), 'The sole thought of being exposed to heights gives me anxiety.', 'I get scared when I stand on high buildings or bridges.'. Cronbach's alpha was calculated to assess the internal consistency of the items, which showed a high consistency of $\alpha = .86$. Lastly, the Affinity for Technology Interaction (ATI) scale by Franke et al. (2019) was used, consisting of nine items, namely: 'I like to occupy myself in greater detail with technical systems.', 'I like testing the functions of new technical systems.', 'I predominantly deal with technical systems because I have to.', 'When I have a new technical system in front of me, I try it out intensively.', 'I enjoy spending time becoming acquainted with a new technical system.', 'It is enough for me that a technical system works; I don't care how or why.', 'I try to understand how a technical system exactly works.', 'It is enough for me to know the basic functions of a technical system.' and 'I try to make full use of the capabilities of a technical system.'. Cronbach's alpha was calculated to assess the internal consistency of the ATI scale, which showed a high consistency with $\alpha = .89$. The items were rated on a 7-point Likert scale from 1 = 'do not agree at all' to 7 = 'totally agree'.

4.2.4 Trust towards the embodied AI

To measure the participant's trust towards the embodied AI, the scale developed by Choudhury and Shamszare (2023) with the three subscales 'trust', 'intent to use' and 'actual use' was implemented and adjusted to fit the context, i.e., 'ChatGPT' was changed to 'AI Assistant'. The participants were instructed to rate the following statements regarding their experience with the embodied AI they just interacted with. The seven items for the subscale 'trust' were: 'The AI Assistant was competent in providing the information and guidance I need.', 'The AI Assistant was reliable in providing consistent and dependable information., 'The AI Assistant was transparent.', 'The AI Assistant was trustworthy in the sense that it is dependable and credible.', 'The AI Assistant did not cause harm, manipulate its responses, create negative consequences for me.', 'The AI Assistant acted with integrity and was honest with me.', 'The AI Assistant was secure and protected my privacy and confidential information.'. The items were randomized to mitigate sequence effects and an attention check was added to ensure participants actually read through the items and did not just click through them, i.e., 'Please select 'fully agree'. The internal consistency was good with $\alpha = .80$. The subscale 'Intent to Use' consists of three items: 'I am willing to use the AI Assistant for healthcare related queries.', 'I am willing to take decisions based on the recommendations provided by the AI Assistant.', 'I am willing to use the AI Assistant in the future.'. Cronbach's alpha was high with α = .88. Additionally, the third subscale 'Actual Use' was implemented with the question 'How frequently do you use ChatGPT or comparable AI Chatbots?' with the answer choices 'Once a month', 'Once a week', 'Many times a week', 'Once a day', Many times a day', 'I have never interacted with ChatGPT.' in a single choice answering format.

4.2.5 Perception of the embodied AI and Intended Self-Disclosure

To measure the perception of the embodied AI, the Godspeed Indices originally developed by Bartneck et al. (2009) and specifically the German translation by Giuliani et al. (2013) was implemented (see Table 4.1). They were all to be rated on a 5-point semantic differential.

Table 4.1 Items of the Godspeed Indices subscales with Cronbach's alpha values

Subscale	Items	α
Anthropomorphism	fake—natural	.73
	machinelike—humanlike	
	unconscious—conscious	
	moving rigidly—moving elegantly	
Animacy	dead—alive	.76
	stagnant—lively	
	mechanical—organic	
	artificial—lifelike	
	inert—interactive	
	apathetic—responsive	
Sympathy	dislike—like	.80
	unfriendly—friendly	
	unkind—kind	
	unpleasant—pleasant	
	awful—nice	

(continued)

Table 4.1 (continued)

Subscale	Items	α
Perceived Intelligence	incompetent—competent	.77
	ignorant—knowledgeable	
	irresponsible—responsible	
	unintelligent—intelligent	
	foolish—sensitive	
Perceived Security	anxious—relaxed	.23
	calm—agitated (R)	
	quiescent—surprised (R)	

The items 'artificial'—'lifelike' in the Anthropomorphism subscale were excluded to avoid confusion as they appear in the Animacy subscale and otherwise appear twice. Moreover, the eeriness subscale of the Uncanny Valley Scale was employed, developed by Ho and MacDorman (2017). Participants were asked to rate their impression of the embodied AI in VR on the following eight items on a 5-point semantic differential: 'reassuring—eerie', 'numbering—freaky', 'ordinary—supernatural', 'unemotional—hair-rising', 'uninspiring—spine-tingling', 'boring—shocking', 'predictable—thrilling', 'bland—uncanny'. The internal consistency for the eeriness subscale was low with $\alpha = .51$.

To assess participants' perception after the interaction, the Positive and Negative Affect Scale (PANAS) developed by Watson et al. (1988) was utilized with ten items for each Affect, which were to be rated on a 5-point Likert scale reaching from 1 = 'not at all' to 5 = 'extremely'. The adjectives describing positive affect were the following 'enthusiastic', 'interested', 'determined', 'excited', 'inspired', 'alert', 'active', 'strong', 'proud' and 'attentive'; whereas the negative Affect items were 'scared', 'afraid', 'upset', 'distressed', 'jittery', 'nervous', 'ashamed', 'guilty', 'irritable', and 'hostile'. The positive ($\alpha = .87$) and negative ($\alpha = .81$) subscale both showed high internal consistency.

Research has previously shown a discrepancy in intended or perceived and actual self-disclosure, mediated by the perceived salience or shame regarding a specific topic, which might alter the outcome of therapy (Farber, 2003; Norberg et al., 2007). Therefore, in addition to the self-disclosure measured through the VR Questionnaires, there are three self-created items implemented into the computer-based questionnaire after the interaction, where participants were asked to think back to the interaction with the embodied AI and their disclosure in VR and rate the following statements on a 7-point Likert scale reaching from 1 =

'do not agree at all' to 7 = ' fully agree': 'I have provided all information openly and honestly.', 'I gave away as much information about myself as intended.', 'I revealed more information than I actually wanted to during the interaction with the AI. (R)'. The three items showed an overall low internal consistency of $\alpha =$ .48.

4.2.6 Debriefing of the purpose of the study

Finally, a debriefing was provided, informing the participants about the manipulation and purpose of the study: 'The aim of this study is to explore what impact detailed information about the AI used and increased control over the use of your data has on your attitudes and trust towards AI and how this influences your information disclosure. The questions in virtual reality are only relevant to provide insight into how much information you would share with an AI. The exact content of your answers are not relevant for the analysis of this study. In addition, your selection for data processing was used to assess how you would share your data. Your data, which was requested before the interaction, was not forwarded to the AI as part of this study and therefore had no influence on your interaction with the AI. Furthermore, the information you shared with the AI will not be passed on to OpenAI, as it was disclosed within a protected university account. OpenAI only analyses metadata about usage, but no content information. The storage of information in your patient file is also beyond our capabilities. Therefore, no information that you have provided as part of this study has been stored in your patient file, even if you have given your consent. If you have any further questions, please contact the experimenter.'

4.3 Results Main Study

The following section provides the results, starting with the Descriptives for the participants' fear of heights, ATI, Trust towards the AI and the Perception of the AI. Moreover, the Manipulation Check and the results of the postulated hypotheses are presented, followed by additional post-hoc calculations.

4.3.1 Descriptives

A total of $N = 90$ participants took part in the study. As the study was a controlled lab-study and appropriate data input was supervised by the experimenter, no participants had to be excluded. The previous experience regarding fear of heights for the $N = 90$ participants showed a Mean of $M = 2.32$ and a Standard Deviation of $SD = 1.21$. The Affinity for Technology (ATI) scale indicated a Mean of $M = 4.00$ and $SD = 1.19$. A total of $n = 3$ (3.3%) participants indicated to have never interacted with ChatGPT before, whereas $n = 15$ (16.7%) interact with it once a month, $n = 19$ (21.1%) once a week, $n = 25$ (27.8%) more than once a week, $n = 8$ (8.9%) participants interact with it once a day and $n = 20$ (22.2%) indicated to interact with ChatGPT more than once a day. The Trust towards the AI scale showed a Mean value of $M = 5.64$ and $SD = 0.85$, whereas the Intention to Use was $M = 4.16$ and $SD = 1.51$. The values for the perception of the embodied AI, i.e., Godspeed Indices and eeriness subscale of the Uncanny Valley scale and the PANAS scale can be found in Table 4.2.

Table 4.2 Mean and Standard Deviation of Perception of the embodied AI

Scale	*M*	*SD*
Trust towards the AI	5.64*	0.85*
Godspeed Indices		
Anthropomorphism	2.31	0.72
Animacy	2.76	0.67
Sympathy	4.10	0.62
Perceived Intelligence	4.10	0.54
Perceived Security	4.32	0.40
Uncanny Valley—eeriness	2.54	0.41
PANAS		
Positive Subscale	2.98	0.70
Negative Subscale	1.28	0.37

Note. * Trust towards the AI was rated on a 7-point Likert scale, whereas every other scale was rated on a 5-point semantic differential.

4.3.2 Manipulation Check

The manipulation of Transparency and Autonomy is assessed through two independent measures T-tests between the respective conditions and the legal condition. The $N = 90$ participants were randomly assigned to one of the three conditions. There were two participants who did not answer the item regarding the check for the autonomy manipulation, therefore each condition has a total of $n = 29$ participants, who answered the respective item. The comparison of the legal condition (1) and the autonomy condition (2) showed a significant Levene's test ($F(1, 56) = 7.19$, $p = .010$), therefore the assumption of homogeneity of variance for the two groups is not met and the results for the Welch's test correction for unequal variances is reported. The t-test showed significantly higher values of perceived autonomy for the autonomy condition ($M = 6.55$, $SD = 0.69$) compared to the legal condition ($M = 5.90$, $SD = 1.70$), $t(36.91) = 1.93$, $p = .030$, $d = 1.29$, 95% CI [−1.34, 0.03].

The homogeneity of variances can be assumed for the legal and transparency condition for $n = 30$ participants in each group, ($F(1, 58) = 3.35$, $p = .072$). The perceived transparency values are significantly higher for the transparency condition ($M = 6.57$, $SD = 0.73$) compared to the legal condition ($M = 5.97$, $SD = 1.47$), $t(58) = 2.00$, $p = .025$, $d = 1.16$, 95% CI [−1.20, 0.00]. Therefore, the manipulation check is successful for the manipulation of both autonomy and transparency.

4.3.3 Autonomy, Transparency and Self-Disclosure

The $n = 30$ participants in the autonomy condition indicated varying choices for the autonomy questions within the computer-based questionnaire. 93.3% ($n = 28$) agreed to their name being passed on, whereas 6.7% ($n = 2$) disagreed. A total of 100% ($n = 30$) selected 'Yes' for the passing on of their age as well as their gender, their previous experience regarding fear of heights to improve the therapeutic interaction with the embodied AI and the participation and information regarding the VR therapy session. 30% ($n = 9$) additionally agreed on the participation and data shared during the session to be saved within their patient folder, while 70% ($n = 21$) declined.

H1: For the following statistical analysis of self-disclosure, the answers to the sensitive questions in the VR questionnaire as well as the items on intended self-disclosure in the computer-based questionnaire are observed. Apart from a general Mean for the sensitive questions, two separate Means were calculated for the first three questions and the remaining three questions as they differ in level of sensibility. To test the effect of autonomy on self-disclosure an independent-measures t-test was conducted. The homogeneity of variances can be assumed for the legal ($n = 30$) and autonomy ($n = 29$) condition, ($F(1, 57) = 0.07$, $p = .789$). There is a significant difference in answers for all sensitive questions between the legal condition ($M = 3.28$, $SD = 0.60$) and the autonomy condition ($M = 3.86$, $SD = 0.62$), $t(57) = 3.65$, $p < .001$, $d = 0.61$, 95% CI [0.90, 0.26]. The first set of sensitive questions (see Fig. 4.12) also shows a significant difference in answers between the legal ($M = 4.98$, $SD = 1.05$) and the autonomy condition ($M = 5.66$, $SD = 0.87$), $t(57) = 2.67$, $p = .010$, $d = 0.97$, 95% CI [1.18, 0.17]. The second set of sensitive questions (see Fig. 4.13), i.e., higher sensibility questions show no significant differences between the legal ($n = 29$, $M = 1.51$, $SD = 0.65$) and autonomy ($n = 28$, $M = 1.94$, $SD = 1.08$) condition for a two-sided comparison, $t(44.06) = 1.83$, $p = .074$, $d = 0.89$, 95% CI [0.91, 0.04]. The Welch's correction is reported as the homogeneity of variances cannot be assumed as a significant Levene's test suggests, $F(55) = 5.55$, $p = .022$. Moreover, the perceived self-disclosure during the interaction with the embodied AI had an overall Mean of $M = 5.01$ and $SD = 0.42$. There are no differences in intended self- disclosure between the legal ($M = 4.97$, $SD = 0.43$) and the autonomy condition ($M = 5.01$, $SD = 0.28$) with $n = 30$ participants each, $t(58) = 0.47$, $p = .639$, $d = 0.37$, 95% CI [0.23, 0.15].

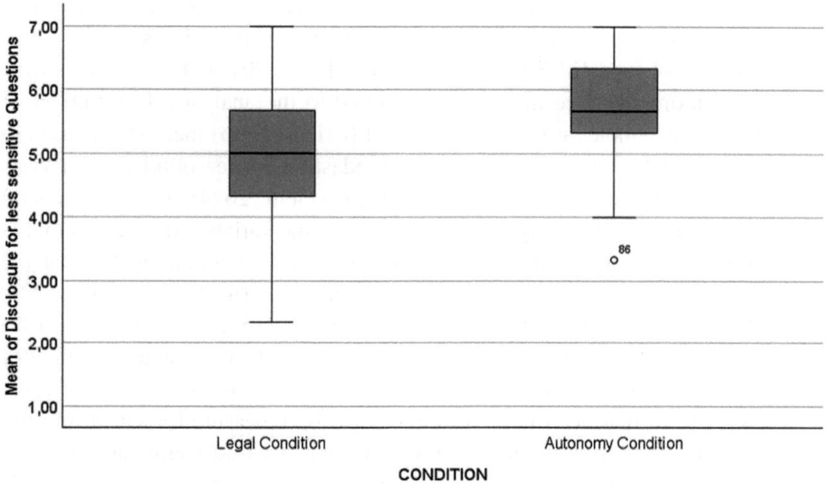

Fig. 4.12 Two boxplots showing significant differences in Mean of disclosure for the less sensitive questions between legal and autonomy condition

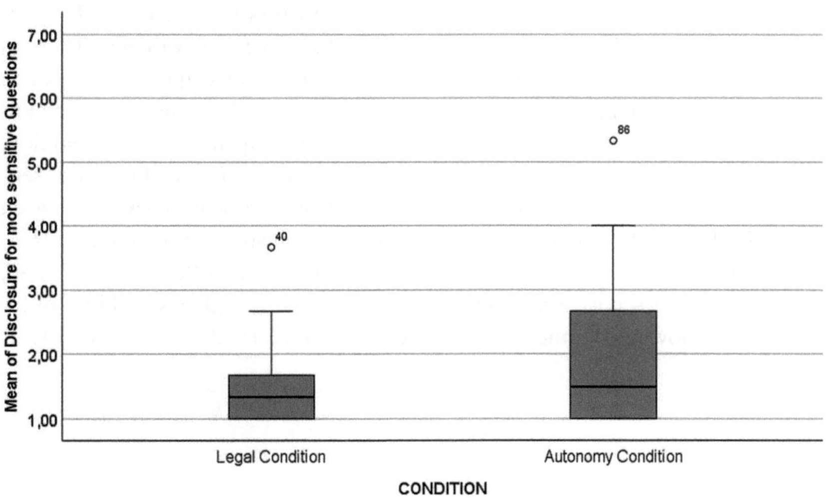

Fig. 4.13 Two boxplots showing non-significant differences in Mean for the higher sensitive questions between legal and autonomy condition

H2: The effect of trust towards the AI on the relationship between autonomy and self-disclosure is examined in a moderator analysis using the PROCESS tool for IBM SPSS Statistic (see Hayes, 2017). The variables trust and autonomy were mean centered prior to the analysis. The number of bootstrap samples was 5000. The HC4 (Cribari-Neto) method was used to adjust for the prerequisite of heteroscedasticity. The confidence intervals are bias-corrected and accelerated (BCa) (Field, 2024). With the general Mean of the sensitive questions as the outcome variable, the overall model was not significant, $F(3, 82) = 1.00$, $p = .397$, explaining 2.7% of the variance. There was no main effect for autonomy ($t(82) = 1.23$, $p = .222$, 95% BCa CI [–0.04, 0.16]) or trust ($t(82) = -0.59$, $p = .559$, 95% BCa CI [–0.20, 0.11]). The results also show no significant interaction effect of trust and autonomy on self-disclosure, $\Delta R^2 = 1.14\%$, $F(1, 82) = 0.57$, $p = .451$. To further determine this effect, a second measure for self-disclosure was observed as a predictor. However, there was no significant effect of the overall model using intended self- disclosure, $R^2 = 8.3\%$, $F(3, 83) = 0.65$, $p = .585$ and no interaction effect between trust and autonomy, $\Delta R^2 = 3.38\%$, $F(1, 83) = 0.04$, $p = .846$.

H3: An independent-measures t-test was additionally employed to determine the effect of transparency on self-disclosure with transparency as the independent variable and self-disclosure as the dependent variable. There is no significant difference in answers for all sensitive questions between the legal condition ($M = 3.28$, $SD = 0.60$) and the transparency condition ($M = 3.56$, $SD = 0.73$) with $n = 30$ participants in each condition, $t(58) = 1.57$, $p = .121$, $d = 0.67$, 95% CI [0.62, 0.07]. The first set of sensitive questions also shows no significant difference in answers between the legal ($M = 4.98$, $SD = 1.05$) and the transparency condition ($M = 5.29$, $SD = 1.07$), $t(58) = 1.12$, $p = .269$, $d = 1.06$, 95% CI [0.85, 0.24]. The second set of sensitive questions, i.e., higher sensibility questions show no significant difference between the legal ($n = 29$, $M = 1.51$,

$SD = 0.65$) and transparency ($n = 29$, $M = 1.68$, $SD = 0.89$) condition, $t(56) = 0.842$, $p = .403$, $d = 0.78$, 95% CI [0.58, 0.24]. There are no differences in intended self-disclosure between the legal ($M = 4.97$, $SD = 0.43$) and the transparency condition ($M = 5.04$, $SD = 0.51$) with $n = 30$ participants each, $t(58) = 0.47$, $p = .526$, $d = 0.37$, 95% CI [0.32, 0.17].

4.3.4 Trust towards the AI

H4: To determine the effect of higher transparency on trust towards the AI, an independent-measures t-test was conducted. The trust towards the AI was not significantly higher in the transparency condition ($M = 5.47$, $SD = 0.84$) compared to the legal condition ($M = 5.58$, $SD = 0.96$) with $n = 30$ participants in each condition, $t(58) = 0.47$, $p = .320$, $d = 0.90$, 95% CI [0.58, 0.36] (see Fig. 4.14 for trust between all three conditions).

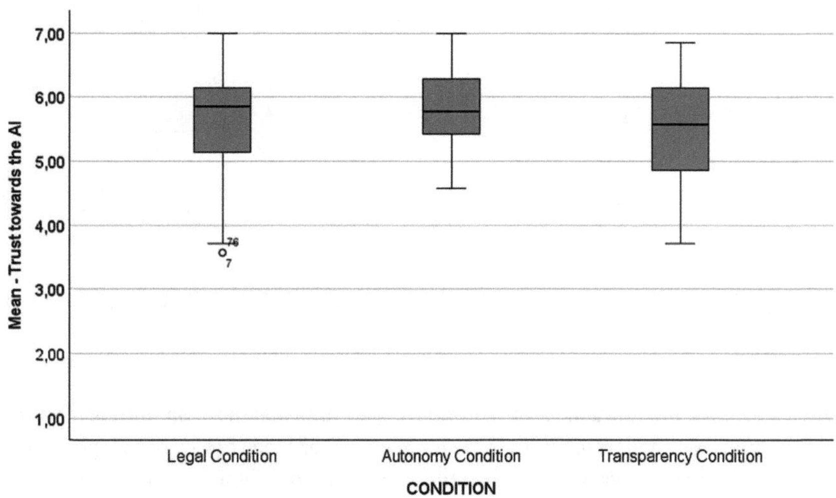

Fig. 4.14 Three boxplots showing non-significant differences in Mean for trust between the three conditions

4.3.5 Perception of the embodied AI and Perceived Safety

H5: The comparison of the effect autonomy and transparency have on positive affect compared to the legal condition is tested through a one-way independent-measures Anova. There is no significant difference between the legal (M = 2.91, SD = 0.75), autonomy (M = 2.98, SD = 0.66) and transparency (M = 3.06, SD = 0.71) condition, $F(2, 87) = 0.307$, p = .736, $\eta^2 = 0.01$ (see Fig. 4.15).

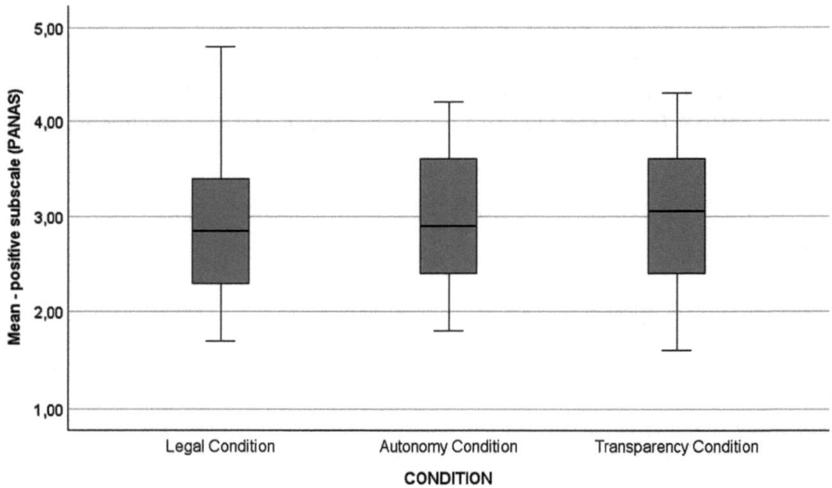

Fig. 4.15 The values for the positive affect subscale between the three conditions

H6: To test the influence of autonomy and transparency on the perceived safety on the terrace with the embodied AI, another one-way independent-measures Anova was conducted. There was no significant difference for perceived safety between the legal condition (M = 6.40, SD = 0.97), the autonomy condition (M = 6.40, SD = 0.89) and the transparency condition (M = 6.60, SD = 0.72), $F(2, 87) = 0.530$, p = .590, η^2 = 0.012.

4.3.6 Post-Hoc Calculations

Based on the previous findings, respective variables and effects on other components are explored further. To determine predictors of trust towards the AI, after excluding possible predictors through explorative statistical analysis an independent- measures t-test was conducted to determine the effect of gender on trust. Participants only selected to be either male or female. The results show that women (M = 5.73, SD = 0.87) had significantly higher trust towards the AI compared to men (M = 5.37, SD = 0.74), $t(88) = 1.75$, $p = .042$, $d = 0.84$ (see Fig. 4.16). Moreover, a Multiple Linear Regression was conducted with the dependent variable perceived safety on the terrace and various predictors, namely fear of heights, previous experience with ChatGPT, ATI, perceived autonomy and perceived transparency were included. The overall model is significant, $F(5, 81) = 2.38$, $p = .046$, explaining 12.8% of variance. However, only fear of heights was a significant negative predictor ($\beta = -0.35$) for perceived safety on the terrace, $t(86) = -3.23$, $p = .002$, whereas the other predictors did not significantly predict perceived safety.

The predictors for the PANAS scale were further explored in two separate Multiple Linear Regressions for each subscale with the predictors fear of heights, previous use, ATI and perceived autonomy and transparency. The model for the negative affect subscale was non-significant, $F(5, 81) = 2.05$, $p = .081$, explaining 11.2% of variance. Previous use of ChatGPT was a significant negative predictor ($\beta = -0.28$) for negative affect, thus higher values of previous use predicted lower negative affect after the interaction, $t(86) = -2.43$, $p = .018$. The same predictors for the positive affect subscale resulted in a non-significant model, $F(5, 81) = 0.61$, $p = .694$, explaining 3.6% of variance. There was no significant predictor for the positive affect subscale.

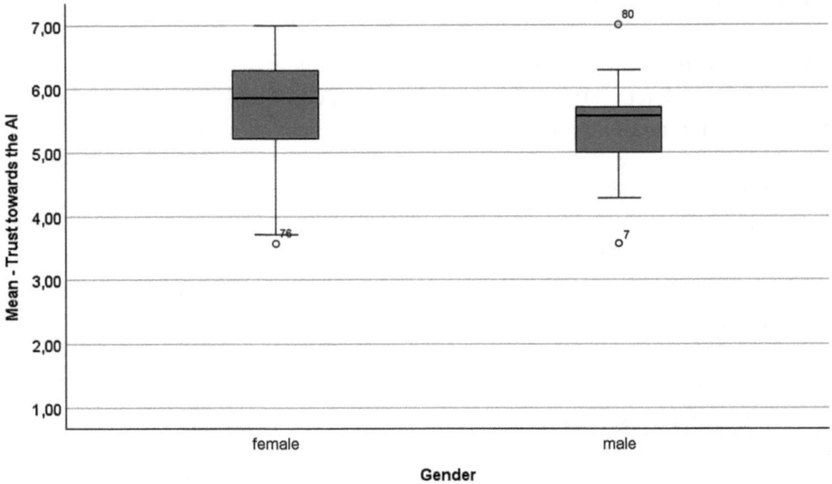

Fig. 4.16 The significant difference in Mean of trust between female and male participants

4.4 Discussion Main Study

The following section discusses the findings of the main study in the order of calculations. Additionally, further findings as well as methodical procedure and study design is discussed, followed by implications for future studies.

4.4.1 Manipulation Check

The manipulation check for both transparency and autonomy were successful. This underlines the effect of providing more choices about participants' collection and processing of data on perceived control, while more information about data collection and the AI increases perceived transparency. It additionally puts into question the level of legally necessary information and provided choices when interacting with AI, regulated through the GDPR and EU AI Act (European Parliament, 2016; European Parliament, 2024). Even a small increase in provided control and transparency over data collection when interacting with AI as done in this study can have effects on e.g., perceived control.

4.4.2 Autonomy, Transparency and Self-Disclosure

The answers to the choices given within the autonomy condition show a generally large readiness to share personal information with the embodied AI. Every person selected the respective information to be passed on, except for a few people who disagreed with the passing on of their name. The openness, particularly in anonymous interactions to share personal data is in line with previous research (see Joinson et al., 2010; Pickard et al., 2016) and can partially be explained by less expected judgment (Kim et al., 2021). A notable amount declined for information to be passed on to their medical patient file. Although the computer-based questionnaire entailed no questions on any medical data, like the name of the participants' insurance company, the question may have been mediated by recent developments in Germany regarding the electronic patient file, which has been passed January 2025, relatively close to the time of this study (Bundesärztekammer, 2024). It is important to note that many participants asked the experimenter to clarify the meaning of the question about information being saved in their patient file. Despite Autonomy and Transparency showing up as separate ethical principles (Fiske et al., 2019; Obremski & Wienrich, 2024), these findings underline the approach of exploring the interdependence of the two principles. Future studies could thus research the effect of providing further information directly when giving users an option to decide on the collection of their data.

H1: The condition with higher **autonomy** regarding one's data results in higher **self-disclosure** compared to the legal condition.

The values for the sensitive questions in the VR questionnaire showed a significant difference between the condition with higher data autonomy and the condition providing only the minimum level of choice in data collection. The self-disclosure within this study was measured through queries about personal information, such as the relationship with one's parents, satisfaction with work or more sensitive questions, asking about alcohol consumption or sexual behavior. It is important to consider the participant pool deployed for this study, which consisted mostly of students at a university who might overall score lower on extreme behavior. While the content is not relevant to the analysis of self-disclosure, e.g., higher autonomy does not predict higher alcohol use, the means of the answers were conducted as the answering behavior should not differ between groups. Additionally, higher values for the sensitive questions do not necessarily suggest higher self-disclosure. It is possible that autonomy had an opposing effect on self-disclosure, causing participants to answer differently based on an increased awareness that their answers would be passed on, i.e., social desirability bias (Connors et al., 2019; Grimm, 2010). When looking at the sets of questions separately, the questions discussing topics higher in sensibility, i.e., alcohol, aggression and sexual behavior, did not significantly differ, whereas means for the less sensitive questions differed significantly. The way the questions were phrased ('I often have aggressive thoughts.', 'I often consume alcohol.') suggests a higher vulnerability and openness with higher values, therefore, the non-significant results for higher sensitive questions are in line with the fear of judgment that oftentimes decreases self-disclosure (Kim et al., 2021). As the values for the second group are still descriptively higher for the autonomy condition and as the manipulation check of autonomy appears to be successful, it is assumed that autonomy increases self-disclosure behavior. Therefore, the first hypothesis is *accepted*. Moreover, the perceived self-disclosure measured after the interaction did not reflect the observed difference in answer behavior for the sensitive questions. It partially underlines the privacy paradox discussed by Norberg et al. (2007), stating that oftentimes intended or perceived self-disclosure differs from actual self-disclosure. On the other hand, this study did not measure the disclosure exhibited during the interaction with the embodied AI, which might possibly reflect the perceived self-disclosure measured in the computer-based questionnaire. The difference in disclosure for more sensitive topics with the embodied AI is comparable to the self-disclosure observed in human therapist interactions as certain sensitive topics are not discussed or lied about, i.e., covert processes (Blanchard & Farber, 2016; Farber & Hall, 2002; Weiner & Shuman, 1984). Henretty and Levitt (2010) additionally point out the possible positive effects of therapist self-disclosure on patient self-disclosure.

H2: The amount of **trust towards the AI** moderates the strength of the relationship between **autonomy** and the amount of **self-disclosure**.

The relationship between autonomy and self-disclosure was further examined through a moderator analysis with trust. No main or interaction effect could be observed between the three variables for neither actual nor perceived self-disclosure. Therefore, the second hypothesis is *rejected*. These findings suggest that the effect of autonomy is not dependent on the level of trust participants feel towards the embodied AI. There appears to be no difference in the impact of autonomy on self-disclosure for differing levels of trust. This contradicts various studies, emphasizing the relevance of trust for self-disclosure (Farber et al., 2004; Lee et al., 2024; Wheeless & Grotz; 1977). However, interacting with a virtual entity might lead to higher perceived anonymity during the interaction, which has positive effects on the participants' self-disclosure, resulting in less perceived judgment. The lack of an effect on trust, or the detection thereof, in this use case supports the aim to employ AI and VR in mental health care. Despite the importance of the therapist-patient bond (Luborsky et al., 1985), an embodied AI might have the advantage of still allowing users to disclose issues openly without having to implement costly trust-fostering mechanisms and thus still lead to a desired therapy outcome. The role of anthropomorphism of human-like AI agents for self-disclosure and trust has been discussed in various studies (e.g., Schuetzler et al., 2018) and although a lower level of human-likeliness can decrease perceived judgment, certain scenarios like when interpersonal support is needed humans were preferred over AI (Kim et al., 2022). The importance of trust in the discussion of highly sensitive topics in AI-controlled therapy should thus be researched further. Hancock et al. (2011) have also suggested the effect of performance-based factors to possibly be of higher relevance for trust than the human-likeness of a system.

H3: The condition with higher **transparency** regarding the AI's function and data protection results in higher **self-disclosure** compared to the legal condition.

The self-disclosure was additionally compared between the transparency and legal condition. However, the results suggest no effect of higher transparency on a higher level of self-disclosure. There was also no effect for different levels of sensibility of questions or perceived self-disclosure. Therefore, the third hypothesis is *rejected*. Whereas the information provided in the transparency condition elaborates on the topic of data encryption and collection, it appears to not directly affect answer behavior for the sensitive questions in VR. The manipulation check for transparency underlines the effect of increased provided information on perceived informativeness, however, it is not clear what type of information exactly would lead to an increase in self-disclosure during the interaction with an AI. The non-significant differences between transparency and legal condition could additionally validate the legally necessary implications of the GDPR and EU AI ACT (European Parliament, 2016; European Parliament, 2024) and that a minimum level of provided information elicits a similar amount of self-disclosure compared to an increased level of transparency. Wienrich and Obremski (2024) also discuss the possible disillusionment of AI through increased transparency, resulting in lower perceived intelligence of the AI. Therefore, the effects of transparency and the exact information that should be provided needs to be re-evaluated.

4.4.3 Trust towards the AI

H4: The condition with higher **transparency** regarding the AI's function and data protection results in higher **trust towards the AI** compared to the legal condition.

The comparison of the transparency and legal condition shows no difference in trust towards the AI, underlining effects around trust and transparency discussed previously. Therefore, the fourth hypothesis is also *rejected*. The descriptive values for trust in the transparency condition were even slightly lower than the trust values observed in the legal condition. This emphasizes the disillusionment of AI as mentioned by Wienrich and Obremski (2024). Generally, although providing users with more information follows ethical guidelines and allows more context for the interpretation of the AI's generated output, higher transparency might have an opposing effect on trust and perceived safety when using the systems as it triggers concerns about data users may not have been aware of otherwise (Adjerid et al., 2013).

4.4.4 Perception of the embodied AI and Perceived Safety

Descriptives as a stand-alone measure are difficult to interpret, however, the subscales of the Godspeed Indices notably differ in value. Whereas the scales Sympathy, Intelligence and Security are relatively high (around $M = 4$ on a 5-point semantic differential), the scales of Anthropomorphism and Animacy are well below the value of 3. This suggests no decrease in perceived sympathy and perceived security in the interaction with the embodied AI, despite notable shortcomings regarding human-likeness and liveliness. Previous research has explored the effect of anthropomorphism of virtual entities and partially suggests no negative effects of lower anthropomorphism, e.g., no effect on participants' behavioural trust (Kulms & Kopp, 2019). Although the Media Equation and CASA paradigm (Nass et al., 1994; Reeves & Nass, 1996) elaborate on the transfer of interpersonal social expectations in human-human interaction onto HCI, it might not necessarily imply negative effects on the perception of the virtual entity when these expectations are not met.

H5: The two conditions with higher **autonomy** and higher **transparency** result in higher positive affect compared to the legal condition.

Additional measures were included to determine the effect of ethical principles on the perception of the embodied AI and affect after the interaction. Although autonomy and transparency descriptively show higher values for positive affect, there is no statistically significant difference between the three conditions. Therefore, the fifth hypothesis is also *rejected*. This result appears to weaken the previous postulation that autonomy and transparency might have a negative effect, at least for the level of perception as an increase in provided information and control does not seem to trigger intense negative emotions.

H6: The two conditions with higher **autonomy** and higher **transparency** lead to higher perceived safety with the embodied AI at the exposure level compared to the legal condition.

The overall aim is the deployment of new technologies for the treatment of mental health disorders, therefore, an item measuring perceived safety on the virtual terrace was implemented. The manipulations did not lead to any statistically significant differences in perceived safety, therefore, the sixth hypothesis is *rejected*. It is important to note that participants were not under instruction to spend a lot of time on the terrace or engage with the environment. Additionally, the user is spawned at the further end of the terrace but still a small distance away from the edge, thus it may not have strongly affected users' feeling of safety. It would be interesting to explore the effect of inclusion of ethical principles on perceived safety in more anxiety-inducing scenarios. The values of perceived safety were descriptively very high, i.e., 6.4 on a 7-point Likert scale. The following additional calculations also explore perceived safety in more detail.

4.4.5 Post-Hoc Calculations

Apart from the calculations done for the assessment of the formulated hypotheses, a few additional variables were explored. Neither transparency nor autonomy had any effect on trust, therefore, other predictors were observed. Specifically, gender appeared to influence trust towards the embodied AI with women having significantly higher trust values compared to men. This effect could possibly be explained through a level of perceived ingroup as the virtual agent is also female-coded. Research has already shown ingroup cues to have a positive effect on rapport between interlocutors, even with a virtual agent as the counterpart (Balliet et al., 2014; Obremski et al., 2023). It would thus suggest that the embodied AI is perceived as a woman and possibly therefore part of one's ingroup rather than just being perceived as a digital entity, which further underlines the Media Equation theory (Nass et al., 1994; Reeves & Nass, 1996).

Moreover, potential variables predicting the perceived safety when standing on the terrace in the virtual environment were tested. Whereas other variables did not have any predicting effects on perceived safety, the fear of heights measure assessed prior to the interaction had a significant effect on safety with high levels in fear of heights negatively predicting perceived safety values. In turn, lower levels of fear of height showed significantly higher perceived safety. Although it can be expected that participants with higher fear of heights would feel less secure on a high building, this validates the realism of the virtual environment and its ability to induce discomfort or the lack thereof, which is relevant for future implication of environments for VRET.

Regarding the perception of the interaction the positive and negative affect subscales were investigated in more detail. The previous use of ChatGPT was a significant predictor for negative affect, suggesting that more previous experience with ChatGPT resulted in significantly lower negative affect. Previous use explained around 12% of the variance of negative affect values with a total of five predictors. The positive affect subscale was, however, not significantly influenced by participants' previous experience with ChatGPT. The findings are in line with the habituation theory, suggesting that repeated exposure to a stimulus decreases discomfort (Rankin et al., 2009). Moreover, negative feelings are more susceptible to this effect, which might explain the lack of a comparable effect for positive affect. Additionally, the topics initiated by the embodied AI during the interaction are not particularly sensitive or should trigger extensive negative emotions. There is also no strong exposure to an anxiety-inducing stimulus and people with strong fear of heights were asked to refrain from participation, therefore, positive affect might generally be high for the participants. Considering the effect of previous use of ChatGPT on negative affect, future work could explore the influence of initially letting participants interact with ChatGPT before talking to the embodied AI in VR, e.g., like writing an email with a therapist before a therapy appointment. This might act as a positive influence on affect based on the theory of the mere exposure effect (Bornstein, 1989).

4.4.6 Method and Study Design

There were a few variables that influenced the interaction with the embodied AI in VR. The answers of the embodied AI were still very high in latency, often causing breaks in between the conversation or with participants having to repeat their answers.

Additionally, participants had to press a button before talking to the embodied AI, which does not necessarily simulate a real conversation. The dialogue topics itself were due to various reasons not very personal and did not require the participants to speak a lot, which is not usually typical for a therapeutic conversation. There were additional shortcomings within the virtual environment, e.g., bad lighting, badly mixed sound effects, etc., which may have additionally decreased the quality of interaction.

Moreover, although the manipulation checks for both autonomy and transparency were significant, it is not clear whether the manipulation was sufficient in transferring the ethical principles. Future studies should consider more elaborate representations of each principle and the inclusion thereof in the direct application rather than in a separate questionnaire. It is overall also important to consider the pool of participants taken for this study as they were mostly students and thus limit the generalizability of results to other populations.

5 Conclusion and Future Work

This work first assessed concerns and relevant factors for the use of AI and VR in mental health care and thus queried mental health patients on their perception thereof in an exploratory pre-study, exploring the Research Questions:

RQ1: What are the concerns regarding VR and AI in mental health care, specifically regarding data security and how can they be accommodated within further development?

The results of the online questionnaire revealed high concerns regarding the effectiveness of treatment and harm that might be caused through these technologies. As reference patients were shown a short video of an early stage of development of the application. The most relevant factors and highest concerns repeatedly reflected the importance of transparency and autonomy for the use of AI and VR in mental health care. Therefore, the subsequent main study focused on these two principles considering human-centered AI and the prevailing ethical principles in a VR in-person study with an embodied AI, investigating the following Research Questions:

RQ2: How does transparency regarding AI and data collection affect self-disclosure and trust towards the embodied AI?

RQ3: How does autonomy regarding AI and data collection affect self-disclosure and trust towards the embodied AI?

The manipulation of transparency and autonomy had little to no effect on participants' self-disclosure and trust towards the embodied AI. There was a generally

P. Friedrich, *To be healed or to be hacked*, BestMasters,
https://doi.org/10.1007/978-3-658-50067-2_5

high readiness to pass on personal information in the autonomy group and a significant increase of disclosure was observed with higher autonomy compared to the legally necessary level of control over data collection. This effect, however, did not translate to the higher sensitive questions, reflecting effects often found in therapist-patient disclosure regarding sensitive topics. Therefore, H1 is accepted, whereas H2—H6 are rejected.

Further calculations suggest the perception of the embodied AI to be independent of the inclusion of ethical principles. Additionally, the intervention appears to have successfully conveyed a level of realism as ingroup effects during the interaction with the embodied AI and a decreased feeling of safety for participants with higher fear of heights could be observed. Ultimately, this study has a variety of implications for the use of AI and VR in mental health care. First, suggesting that ethical principles are difficult to consider separately and their interdependence should be explored further. Moreover, it underlines the benefits of AI-controlled therapy as the anonymity of the interaction can increase users' self-disclosure and therein provide support in discussing mental health issues without fear of judgment. The lack of effects on self-disclosure and trust encourage the exploration of effects other ethical principles have on different aspects of the interaction.

Future work should consider the implementation of semantic analysis of content of speech to trigger the virtual agent's animations and facial expressions accordingly and thus create a congruent dialogue. The effect of previous experience with ChatGPT on negative affect should not be neglected and possibly incorporated into further study designs. Seeing the importance of suitable applications to support affected people in need, it is crucial to establish safe ways of implementing these tools. Ethical implications have been widely formulated and are encouraged to implement early in the design process. Therefore, more research is necessary to clarify the translation of ethical guidelines into tangible, technological implications. Lastly, the question remains 'To be healed or to be hacked?'.

Despite the risks related to AI, it also allows the possibility of significantly supporting mental health care professionals and providing necessary resources for the large amount of people in need. When properly implementing ethical principles into AI-controlled therapy, users should not have to compromise their safety to get the help they deserve.

Literature

Abbruzzese, E., & Kübler, U. (2013). Verhaltensanalyse in der Verhaltenstherapie. *Verhaltenstherapie, 23*(2), 108–116. https://doi.org/10.1159/000351185

Abiteboul, S., & Stoyanovich, J. (2019). Transparency, fairness, data protection, neutrality: Data management challenges in the face of new regulation. *Journal of Data and Information Quality, 11*(3), 1–9. https://doi.org/10.1145/3310231

Adjerid, I., Acquisti, A., Brandimarte, L., & Loewenstein, G. (2013). Sleights of privacy: Framing, disclosures, and the limits of transparency. In *Proceedings of the ninth symposium on usable privacy and security* (pp. 1–11). https://doi.org/10.1145/2501604.2501613

Aguinis, H., & Henle, C. A. (2004). Ethics in research. *Handbook of research methods in industrial and organizational psychology*, 34–56. https://doi.org/10.1002/9780470756669.ch2

American Psychiatric Association, D. S. M. T. F., & American Psychiatric Association, D. S. (2013). *Diagnostic and statistical manual of mental disorders: DSM-5* (Vol. 5, No. 5). Washington, DC: American psychiatric association.

Angelov, P. P., Soares, E. A., Jiang, R., Arnold, N. I., & Atkinson, P. M. (2021). Explainable artificial intelligence: an analytical review. *Wiley Interdisciplinary Reviews: Data Mining and Knowledge Discovery*, *11*(5), e1424. https://doi.org/10.1002/widm.1424

AOK Presse und Politik. (2024). *ePA-Umfrage zeigt hohe Akzeptanz*. Retrieved November 22, 2024, from https://www.aok.de/pp/gg/update/epa-umfrage-zeigt-hohe-akzeptanz/

AOK Rheinland/Hamburg. (2024). *Elektronische Patientenakte: Informationswege und—bedarfe*. AOK Rheinland/Hamburg. https://www.aok.de/pk/rh/

Auernhammer, J. (2020). Human-centered AI: The role of Human-centered Design Research in the development of AI. https://doi.org/10.21606/drs.2020.282

Balliet, D., Wu, J., & De Dreu, C. K. (2014). Ingroup favoritism in cooperation: a meta-analysis. *Psychological bulletin, 140*(6), 1556–1581. https://doi.org/10.1037/a0037737

Bandelow, B., Lichte, T., Rudolf, S., Wiltink, J., & Beutel, M. (2015). S3-Leitlinie: Kurzfassung der Empfehlungen zur Behandlung von Angststörungen. In B. Bandelow, T. Lichte, S. Rudolf, J. Wiltink, & M. Beutel (Eds.), *S3-Leitlinie Angststörungen*. Springer. https://doi.org/10.1007/978-3-662-44136-7_1

P. Friedrich, *To be healed or to be hacked*, BestMasters,
https://doi.org/10.1007/978-3-658-50067-2

Bandelow, B., Michaelis, S., & Wedekind, D. (2017). Treatment of anxiety disorders. Dialogues in clinical neuroscience, 19(2), 93–107. https://doi.org/10.31887/DCNS.2017.19.2/bbandelow

Bär, N., Hoffmann, A., & Krems, J. (2011). Entwicklung von Testmaterial zur experimentellen Untersuchung des Einflusses von Usability auf Online- Trust. *Reflexionen und Visionen der Mensch-Maschine-Interaktion–Aus der Vergangenheit lernen, Zukunft gestalten, 9.*

Bhugra, D., Till, A., & Sartorius, N. (2013). What is mental health?. *International Journal of Social Psychiatry, 59*(1), 3–4. https://doi.org/10.1177/0020764012463315

Biancardi, B., Cafaro, A., & Pelachaud, C. (2017). Could a virtual agent be warm and competent? investigating user's impressions of agent's non-verbal behaviours. In *Proceedings of the 1st acm sigchi international workshop on investigating social interactions with artificial agents* (pp. 22–24). https://doi.org/10.1145/3139491.3139498

Blanchard, M. & Farber, B. A. (2016). Lying in psychotherapy: Why and what clients don't tell their therapist about therapy and their relationship, *Counselling Psychology Quarterly, 29*(1), 90–112, https://doi.org/10.1080/09515070.2015.1085365

Bornstein, R. F. (1989). Exposure and affect: Overview and meta-analysis of research, 1968–1987. *Psychological bulletin, 106*(2), 265–289. https://psycnet.apa.org/doi/10.1037/0033-2909.106.2.265

Botella, C. M., Juan, M. C., Baños, R. M., Alcañiz, M., Guillén, V., & Rey, B. (2005). Mixing realities? An application of augmented reality for the treatment of cockroach phobia. *Cyberpsychology & behavior, 8*(2), 162–171. https://doi.org/10.1089/cpb.2005.8.162

Bowman, D. A., Kruijff, E., LaViola, J. J., & Poupyrev, I. (2001). An introduction to 3-D user interface design. *Presence, 10*(1), 96–108. https://doi.org/10.1162/105474601750182342

BPtK. (2022). Psychisch Kranke warten 142 Tage auf eine Psychotherapie. Retrieved September 23, 2024, from https://www.bptk.de/pressemitteilungen/psychisch-kranke-warten-142-tage-auf-eine-psychotherapeutische-behandlung/

Brell, T., Philipsen, R., & Ziefle, M. (2019). sCARy! Risk perceptions in autonomous driving: The influence of experience on perceived benefits and barriers. *Risk analysis, 39*(2), 342–357. https://doi.org/10.1111/risa.13190

Brown, T., Mann, B., Ryder, N., Subbiah, M., Kaplan, J. D., Dhariwal, P., ... & Amodei, D. (2020). Language models are few-shot learners. *Advances in neural information processing systems, 33*, 1877–1901. https://doi.org/10.48550/arXiv.2005.14165

Buhalis, D., & Moldavska, I. (2022). Voice assistants in hospitality: using artificial intelligence for customer service. *Journal of Hospitality and Tourism Technology, 13*(3), 386–403. https://doi.org/10.1108/JHTT-03-2021-0104

Bundesärztekammer. (2024). *Elektronische Patientenakte (EPA).* Retrieved November 25, 2024, from https://www.bundesaerztekammer.de/themen/aerzte/digitalisierung/digitale-anwendungen/telematikinfrastruktur/epa

Bundesministerium der Justiz. (2024). *Gesundheitsdatennutzungsgesetz (GDNG).* Gesetze im Internet. Retrieved November 25, 2024, from https://www.gesetze-im-internet.de/gdng/BJNR0660B0024.html

Bundesministerium für Gesundheit. (2023). *Gesundheitsdatennutzungsgesetz (GDNG).* Bundesgesundheitsministerium. Retrieved November 25, 2024, from https://www.bundesgesundheitsministerium.de/ministerium/gesetze-und-verordnungen/guv-20-lp/gesundheitsdatennutzungsgesetz.html

Caldwell, B., Cooper, M., Reid, L. G., Vanderheiden, G., Chisholm, W., Slatin, J., & White, J. (2008). Web content accessibility guidelines (WCAG) 2.0. *WWW Consortium (W3C), 290*(1–34), 5–12. http://www.w3.org/TR/2008/REC-WCAG20-20081211/

Calvo, R. A., Deterding, S., & Ryan, R. M. (2020). Health surveillance during covid-19 pandemic. *BMJ, 369*, Article m1373. https://doi.org/10.1136/bmj.m1373

Chen, X. W., & Lin, X. (2014). Big data deep learning: challenges and perspectives. *IEEE access, 2*, 514–525. https://doi.org/10.1109/ACCESS.2014.2325029

Chignell, M. H., Quan-Haase, A., & Gwizdka, J. (2003). The Privacy Attitudes Questionnaire (PAQ): Initial Development and Validation. *Proceedings of the Human Factors and Ergonomics Society Annual Meeting, 47*(11), 1326–1330. https://doi.org/10.1177/154193120304701102

Child, J. T., Pearson, J. C., & Petronio, S. (2009). Blogging, communication, and privacy management: Development of the Blogging Privacy Management Measure. *Journal of the American Society for Information Science and Technology, 60*(10), 2079–2094. https://doi.org/10.1002/asi.21122

Choudhury, A., & Shamszare, H. (2023). Investigating the impact of user trust on the adoption and use of ChatGPT: survey analysis. *Journal of Medical Internet Research, 25*, e47184. https://doi.org/10.2196/47184

Connors, E. C., Krupnikov, Y., & Ryan, J. B. (2019). How transparency affects survey responses. *Public Opinion Quarterly, 83*(S1), 185–209. https://doi.org/10.1093/poq/nfz013

Cook, M. (1977). Gaze and Mutual Gaze in Social Encounters: How long—and when— we look others" in the eye" is one of the main signals in nonverbal communication. *American Scientist, 65*(3), 328–333. https://www.jstor.org/stable/27847843

Corrigan, P. W., & Rüsch, N. (2002). Mental Illness Stereotypes and Clinical Care: Do People Avoid Treatment Because of Stigma? *Psychiatric Rehabilitation Skills, 6*(3), 312–334. https://doi.org/10.1080/10973430208408441

Crisis Text Line. (2018). *Detecting crisis: An AI solution.* Crisis Text Line. https://www.crisistextline.org/blog/2018/03/28/detecting-crisis-an-ai-solution/

D'Alfonso, S. (2020). AI in mental health. *Current opinion in psychology, 36*, 112–117. https://doi.org/10.1016/j.copsyc.2020.04.005

DAK. (2024). Sick days due taken to mental illness in Germany from 1997 to 2023. In Statista. Retrieved February, 2025, from https://www.statista.com/statistics/1372953/sick-leave-index-mental-illness-germany/

Danks, D., & London, A. J. (2017). Algorithmic Bias in Autonomous Systems. In *Ijcai* (Vol. 17, No. 2017, 4691–4697. https://doi.org/10.24963/ijcai.2017/654

Dastin, J. (2022). *Amazon scraps secret AI recruiting tool that showed bias against women.* In *Ethics of data and analytics* (1st ed., pp. 4). Auerbach Publications. https://doi.org/10.1201/9781003278290

Deci, E. L., & Ryan, R. M. (2012). Self-determination theory. *Handbook of theories of social psychology, 1*(20), 416–436. https://doi.org/10.4135/9781446249215.n21

Delbosc, A., Ochs, M., Sabouret, N., Ravenet, B., & Ayache, S. (2023). Towards the generation of synchronized and believable non-verbal facial behaviors of a talking virtual agent. In *Companion Publication of the 25th International Conference on Multimodal Interaction* (pp. 228–237). https://doi.org/10.1145/3610661.3616547

Deloitte Deutschland. (2024). *Akzeptanz für die elektronische Patientenakte sinkt*. Retrieved November 26, 2024, from https://www.deloitte.com/de/de/about/press-room/Akzeptanz-fuer-die-elektronische-Patientenakte-sinkt.html

Demartini, G., Mizzaro, S., & Spina, D. (2020). Human-in-the-loop Artificial Intelligence for Fighting Online Misinformation: Challenges and Opportunities. *IEEE Data Eng. Bull.*, *43*(3), 65–74.

Difede, J., Cukor, J., Jayasinghe, N., Patt, I., Jedel, S., Spielman, L., ... & Hoffman, H. G. (2007). Virtual reality exposure therapy for the treatment of posttraumatic stress disorder following September 11, 2001. *Journal of clinical psychiatry*, *68*(11), 1639. https://doi.org/10.4088/JCP.v68n1102

Ekinci, K. (2023). *The era of digital health data in Europe—a detailed look at key legislative initiatives*. adesso Blog. https://www.adesso.de/en/news/blog/the-era-of-digital-health-data-in-europe-a-detailed-look-at-key-legislative-initiatives-2.jsp

Emmelkamp, P. M., Krijn, M., Hulsbosch, A. M., de Vries, S., Schuemie, M. J., & van der Mast, C. A. (2002). Virtual reality treatment versus exposure in vivo: a comparative evaluation in acrophobia. *Behaviour research and therapy*, *40*(5), 509–516. https://doi.org/10.1016/s0005-7967(01)00023-7

Ethikrat, D. (2023). Mensch und Maschine-Herausforderungen durch Künstliche Intelligenz. Stellungnahme, Berlin.

European Parliament; Council of the European Union. (2016). Regulation (EU) 2016/679 of 27 April 2016 on the protection of natural persons with regard to the processing of personal data and on the free movement of such data (General Data Protection Regulation). *Official Journal of the European Union, L 119*, 1–88. https://eur-lex.europa.eu/legal-content/EN/TXT/?uri=CELEX%3A32016R0679

European Parliament; Council of the European Union. (2024). Regulation (EU) 2024/789 of 24 March 2024 on artificial intelligence (Artificial Intelligence Act). *Official Journal of the European Union, L 200*, 1–50. https://eur-lex.europa.eu/legal-content/EN/TXT/?uri=CELEX%3A32024R0789

Farber, B. A. (2003). Patient self-disclosure: a review of the research. *Journal of clinical psychology*, *59*(5), 589–600. https://doi.org/10.1002/jclp.10161

Farber, B. A., & Hall, D. (2002). Disclosure to therapists: What is and is not discussed in psychotherapy. *Journal of clinical psychology*, *58*(4), 359–370. https://psycnet.apa.org/doi/10.1002/jclp.1148

Farber, B. A., Berano, K. C., & Capobianco, J. A. (2004). Clients' Perceptions of the Process and Consequences of Self-Disclosure in Psychotherapy. *Journal of Counseling Psychology*, *51*(3), 340. https://psycnet.apa.org/doi/10.1037/0022-0167.51.3.340

Field, A. (2024). *Discovering statistics using IBM SPSS statistics*. Sage publications limited.

Finstad, K. (2010). Response interpolation and scale sensitivity: Evidence against 5-point scales. *Journal of usability studies*, *5*(3), 104–110.

Fiske, A., Henningsen, P., & Buyx, A. (2019). Your robot therapist will see you now: ethical implications of embodied artificial intelligence in psychiatry, psychology, and psychotherapy. *Journal of medical Internet research*, *21*(5), e13216. https://doi.org/10.2196/13216

Foa, E. B., Steketee, G., & Grayson, J. B. (1985). Imaginal and in vivo exposure: A comparison with obsessive-compulsive checkers. *Behavior Therapy*, *16*(3), 292–302. https://doi.org/10.1016/S0005-7894(85)80017-4

Franke, T., Attig, C., & Wessel, D. (2019). A personal resource for technology interaction: development and validation of the affinity for technology interaction (ATI) scale. *International Journal of Human–Computer Interaction, 35*(6), 456–467. https://doi.org/10.1080/10447318.2018.1456150

Freedman, J. L., & Fraser, S. C. (1966). Compliance without pressure: the foot-in-the- door technique. *Journal of personality and social psychology, 4*(2), 195–202. https://psycnet.apa.org/doi/10.1037/h0023552

Furnham, A., & Swami, V. (2018). Mental health literacy: A review of what it is and why it matters. *International Perspectives in Psychology, 7*(4), 240–257. https://doi.org/10.1037/ipp0000094

Fusar-Poli,P., de Pablo, G. S., De Micheli, A., Nieman, D. H., Correll, C. U., Kessing, L. V., ... & van Amelsvoort, T. (2020). What is good mental health? A scoping review. *European neuropsychopharmacology, 31*, 33–46. https://doi.org/10.1016/j.euroneuro.2019.12.105

Gabbard, J. L., Hix, D., & Swan, J. E. (1999). User-centered design and evaluation of virtual environments. *IEEE computer Graphics and Applications, 19*(6), 51–59. https://doi.org/10.1109/38.799740

Garcia-Palacios, A., Hoffman, H., Carlin, A., Furness III, T. A., & Botella, C. (2002). Virtual reality in the treatment of spider phobia: a controlled study. *Behaviour research and therapy, 40*(9), 983–993. https://doi.org/10.1016/s0005-7967(01)00068-7

Gaur, L., Afaq, A., Arora, G. K., & Khan, N. (2023). Artificial intelligence for carbon emissions using system of systems theory. *Ecological Informatics, 76*, Article 102165. https://doi.org/10.1016/j.ecoinf.2023.102165

Gillespie, N., Lockey, S., & Curtis, C. (2021). Trust in artificial intelligence: A five country study. https://doi.org/10.14264/e34bfa3

Glikson, E., & Woolley, A. W. (2020). Human trust in artificial intelligence: Review of empirical research. *Academy of management annals, 14*(2), 627–660. https://doi.org/10.5465/annals.2018.0057

Grimm, P. (2010). Social desirability bias. *Wiley international encyclopedia of marketing.* https://doi.org/10.1002/9781444316568.wiem02057

Groom, V., Nass, C., Chen, T., Nielsen, A., Scarborough, J. K., & Robles, E. (2009). Evaluating the effects of behavioral realism in embodied agents. *International Journal of Human-Computer Studies, 67*(10), 842–849. https://psycnet.apa.org/doi/10.1016/j.ijhcs.2009.07.001

Guéguen, N. (2002). Foot-in-the-door technique and computer-mediated communication. *Computers in Human Behavior, 18*(1), 11–15. https://psycnet.apa.org/doi/10.1016/S0747-5632(01)00033-4

Hancock, J. T., Naaman, M., & Levy, K. (2020). AI-mediated communication: Definition, research agenda, and ethical considerations. *Journal of Computer-Mediated Communication, 25*(1), 89–100. https://psycnet.apa.org/doi/10.1093/jcmc/zmz022

Hancock, P. A., Billings, D. R., Schaefer, K. E., Chen, J. Y. C., de Visser, E. J., & Parasuraman, R. (2011). A Meta-Analysis of Factors Affecting Trust in Human- Robot Interaction. *Human Factors, 53*(5), 517–527. https://doi.org/10.1177/0018720811417254

Hayes, A. F. (2017). *Introduction to mediation, moderation, and conditional process analysis: A regression-based approach.* Guilford publications.

Henretty, J. R., & Levitt, H. M. (2010). The role of therapist self-disclosure in psychotherapy: A qualitative review. *Clinical psychology review, 30*(1), 63–77. https://doi.org/10.1016/j.cpr.2009.09.004

Higgins, E. T., Bargh, J. A., & Lombardi, W. J. (1985). Nature of priming effects on categorization. *Journal of experimental psychology: Learning, Memory, and Cognition, 11*(1), 59–69. https://psycnet.apa.org/doi/10.1037/0278-7393.11.1.59

Ho, C.-C., & MacDorman, K. F. (2017). Measuring the Uncanny Valley Effect: Refinements to Indices for Perceived Humanness, Attractiveness, and Eeriness. *International Journal of Social Robotics, 9*(2), 129–139. https://doi.org/10.1007/s12369-016-0380-9

Høglend, P. (2014). Exploration of the patient-therapist relationship in psychotherapy. *American Journal of Psychiatry, 171*(10), 1056–1066.

Hsiao, C. Y., Lu, H. L., & Tsai, Y. F. (2015). Factors influencing mental health nurses' attitudes towards people with mental illness. International journal of mental health nursing, 24(3), 272–280. https://doi.org/10.1111/inm.12129

IBM. (2025). What is machine learning? *IBM*. https://www.ibm.com/think/topics/machine-learning

Inkster, B., Sarda, S., & Subramanian, V. (2018). An empathy-driven, conversational artificial intelligence agent (Wysa) for digital mental well-being: real-world data evaluation mixed-methods study. *JMIR mHealth and uHealth, 6*(11), e12106. https://doi.org/10.2196/12106

Jeno, L. M., Adachi, R. A., & Deci, E. L. (2019). The effects of m-learning on motivation, achievement and well-being: A Self-Determination Theory approach. *British Journal of Educational Technology, 50*(2), 672–684. https://doi.org/10.1111/bjet.12657

Jerald, J. (2015). *The VR book: Human-centered design for virtual reality*. Morgan & Claypool. https://doi.org/10.1145/2792790

Joinson, A. N., & Paine, C. B. (2007). Self-disclosure, privacy and the Internet. *The Oxford handbook of Internet psychology, 2374252*, 237–252. https://doi.org/10.1093/oxfordhb/9780199561803.013.0016

Joinson, A. N., Reips, U. D., Buchanan, T., & Schofield, C. B. P. (2010). Privacy, Trust, and Self-Disclosure Online. *Human–Computer Interaction, 25*(1), 1–24. https://doi.org/10.1080/07370020903586662

Juan, M. C., Botella, C., Alcaniz, M., Banos, R., Carrion, C., Melero, M., & Lozano, J. A. (2004). An augmented reality system for treating psychological disorders: application to phobia to cockroaches. In *Third ieee and acm international symposium on mixed and augmented reality*, 256–257. IEEE. https://doi.org/10.1109/ISMAR.2004.14

Kaczkurkin, A. N., & Foa, E. B. (2015). Cognitive-behavioral therapy for anxiety disorders: an update on the empirical evidence. Dialogues in clinical neuroscience, 17(3), 337–346. https://doi.org/10.31887/DCNS.2015.17.3/akaczkurkin

Kallinen, K. (2017). The effects of transparency and task type on trust, stress, quality of work, and co-worker preference during human-autonomous system collaborative work. In *Proceedings of the companion of the 2017 ACM/IEEE international conference on human-robot interaction* (pp. 153–154). https://doi.org/10.1145/3029798.3038386

Kang, S. H., & Gratch, J. (2010). Virtual humans elicit socially anxious interactants' verbal self-disclosure. *Computer Animation and Virtual Worlds, 21*(3-4), 473–482. https://doi.org/10.1002/cav.345

Kardong-Edgren, S. S., Farra, S. L., Alinier, G., & Young, H. M. (2019). A call to unify definitions of virtual reality. *Clinical simulation in nursing, 31*, 28–34. https://doi.org/10.1016/j.ecns.2019.02.006

Khan, S., & Iqbal, M. (2020). AI-Powered Customer Service: Does it optimize customer experience?. In *2020 8th International Conference on Reliability, Infocom Technologies and Optimization (Trends and Future Directions)(ICRITO)*, 590–594. IEEE. https://doi.org/10.1109/ICRITO48877.2020.9198004

Kim, J., Giroux, M., & Lee, J. C. (2021). When do you trust AI? The effect of number presentation detail on consumer trust and acceptance of AI recommendations. *Psychology & Marketing, 38*(7), 1140–1155. https://doi.org/10.1002/mar.21498

Kim, T. W., Jiang, L., Duhachek, A., Lee, H., & Garvey, A. (2022). Do you mind if I ask you a personal question? How AI service agents alter consumer self-disclosure. *Journal of Service Research, 25*(4), 649–666. https://doi.org/10.1177/10946705221120232

Kok, J. N., Boers, E. J., Kosters, W. A., Van der Putten, P., & Poel, M. (2009). Artificial intelligence: definition, trends, techniques, and cases. *Artificial intelligence, 1*(51), 270–299. https://coilink.org/20.500.12592/5hqc03v

Kordzadeh, N., & Ghasemaghaei, M. (2021). Algorithmic bias: review, synthesis, and future research directions. *European Journal of Information Systems, 31*(3), 388–409. https://doi.org/10.1080/0960085X.2021.1927212

Krijn, M., Emmelkamp, P. M., Olafsson, R. P., & Biemond, R. (2004). Virtual reality exposure therapy of anxiety disorders: A review. Clinical psychology review, 24(3), 259–281. https://doi.org/10.1016/j.cpr.2004.04.001

Kuhn, J., Gaebel, W., Klosterkoetter, J., & Woopen, C. (2009). Deep brain stimulation as a new therapeutic approach in therapy-resistant mental disorders: ethical aspects of investigational treatment. *European Archives of Psychiatry and Clinical Neuroscience, 259*, 135–141. https://doi.org/10.1007/s00406-009-0055-8

Kulms, P., & Kopp, S. (2019). More human-likeness, more trust? The effect of anthropomorphism on self-reported and behavioral trust in continued and interdependent human-agent cooperation. In *Proceedings of mensch und computer 2019*, 31–42. https://doi.org/10.1145/3340764.3340793

Kupfer, J. (1987). Privacy, autonomy, and self-concept. *American Philosophical Quarterly, 24*(1), 81–89. https://www.jstor.org/stable/20014176

Laacke, S., Mueller, R., Schomerus, G., & Salloch, S. (2021). Artificial intelligence, social media and depression. A new concept of health-related digital autonomy. *The American Journal of Bioethics, 21*(7), 4–20. https://doi.org/10.1080/15265161.2020.1863515

Lacroux, A., & Martin-Lacroux, C. (2022). Should I trust the artificial intelligence to recruit? Recruiters' perceptions and behavior when faced with algorithm-based recommendation systems during resume screening. *Frontiers in Psychology, 13*, Article 895997. https://doi.org/10.3389/fpsyg.2022.895997

Laoutaris, N. (2018). Data transparency: Concerns and prospects [Point of view]. *Proceedings of the IEEE, 106*(11), 1867–1871. https://doi.org/10.1109/JPROC.2018.2872313

Lee, J., Lee, D., & Lee, J. G. (2024). Influence of rapport and social presence with an AI psychotherapy chatbot on users' self-disclosure. *International Journal of Human– Computer Interaction, 40*(7), 1620–1631. https://doi.org/10.1080/10447318.2022.2146227

LitsLink. (2024). *How many jobs will AI take over—The statistics*. LitsLink. Retrieved from https://litslink.com/blog/how-many-jobs-will-ai-take-over-the-statistics

Liu, B. (2021). In AI we trust? Effects of agency locus and transparency on uncertainty reduction in human–AI interaction. *Journal of computer-mediated communication, 26*(6), 384–402. https://doi.org/10.1093/jcmc/zmab013

Long, D., & Magerko, B. (2020). What is AI literacy? Competencies and design considerations. In *Proceedings of the 2020 CHI conference on human factors in computing systems*, 1–16. https://doi.org/10.1145/3313831.3376727

Luborsky, L., McLellan, A. T., Woody, G. E., O'Brien, C. P., & Auerbach, A. (1985). Therapist success and its determinants. *Archives of general psychiatry, 42*(6), 602–611. https://doi.org/10.1001/archpsyc.1985.01790290084010

Margulis, S. T. (2011). Three Theories of Privacy: An Overview. In S. Trepte & L. Reinecke (Hrsg.), *Privacy Online* (S. 9–17). Springer Berlin Heidelberg. https://doi.org/10.1007/978-3-642-21521-6_2

McEwen, B. S. (2008). Central effects of stress hormones in health and disease: Understanding the protective and damaging effects of stress and stress mediators. *European journal of pharmacology, 583*(2–3), 174–185. https://doi.org/10.1016/j.ejphar.2007.11.071

Michelson, L., & Mavissakalian, M. (1985). Psychophysiological outcome of behavioral and pharmacological treatments of agoraphobia. *Journal of Consulting and Clinical Psychology, 53*(2), 229–236. https://doi.org/10.1037/0022-006x.53.2.229

Miller, G. A. (1956). The magic number seven plus or minus two: Some limits on our capacity for processing information. *Psychological review, 63*, 91–97. https://doi.org/10.1037/h0043158

Minh, D., Wang, H. X., Li, Y. F., & Nguyen, T. N. (2022). Explainable artificial intelligence: a comprehensive review. *Artificial Intelligence Review*, 1–66. https://link.springer.com/article/10.1007%2Fs10462-021-10088-y

Mölbert, S. C., Thaler, A., Mohler, B. J., Streuber, S., Romero, J., Black, M. J., ... & Giel, K. E. (2018). Assessing body image in anorexia nervosa using biometric self- avatars in virtual reality: Attitudinal components rather than visual body size estimation are distorted. *Psychological medicine, 48*(4), 642–653. https://doi.org/10.1017/s0033291717002008

Monteith, S., Glenn, T., Geddes, J. R., Whybrow, P. C., Achtyes, E., & Bauer, M. (2024). Artificial intelligence and increasing misinformation. *The British Journal of Psychiatry, 224*(2), 33–35. https://doi.org/10.1192/bjp.2023.136

Montgomery, B. (2024). Mother says AI chatbot led her son to kill himself in lawsuit against its maker. *The Guardian.* https://www.theguardian.com/technology/2024/oct/23/character-ai-chatbot-sewell-setzer-death

Morina, N., Ijntema, H., Meyerbröker, K., & Emmelkamp, P. M. (2015). Can virtual reality exposure therapy gains be generalized to real-life? A meta-analysis of studies applying behavioral assessments. *Behaviour research and therapy, 74*, 18–24. https://doi.org/10.1016/j.brat.2015.08.010

Murdoch, W. J., Singh, C., Kumbier, K., Abbasi-Asl, R., & Yu, B. (2019). Interpretable machine learning: Definitions, methods, and applications. *Proc. Natl. Acad. Sci. U.S.A. 116*(44), 22071–22080. https://doi.org/10.1073/pnas.1900654116

Murel, J., & Noble, J. (2024). What is LLM temperature? IBM. https://www.ibm.com/think/topics/llm-temperature

Nass, C., Steuer, J., & Tauber, E. R. (1994). Computers are social actors. In *Proceedings of the SIGCHI conference on Human factors in computing systems*, 72–78. https://doi.org/10.1145/191666.191703

National Alliance on Mental Illness. (2023). *Mental health by the numbers.* https://www.nami.org/mhstats

Nielsen, J., & Molich, R. (1990). Heuristic evaluation of user interfaces. In *Proceedings of the SIGCHI conference on Human factors in computing systems* (pp. 249–256).

Njoku, I. (2022). What is Mental Illness? https://psychiatry.org/patients-families/what-is-mental-illness

Norberg, P. A., Horne, D. R., & Horne, D. A. (2007). The Privacy Paradox: Personal Information Disclosure Intentions versus Behaviors. *Journal of Consumer Affairs, 41*(1), 100–126. https://doi.org/10.1111/j.1745-6606.2006.00070.x

Obremski, D., & Wienrich, C. (2024). Autonomous VR Exposure Therapy for Anxiety Disorders Using Conversational AI—Ethical and Technical Implications and Preliminary Results. *Journal of Computer and Communications, 12*(4), 111–138. https://doi.org/10.4236/jcc.2024.124010

Obremski, D., Friedrich, P., Schaper, P., & Lugrin, B. (2023). Effects of Social Ingroup Cues on Empathy Towards an Intelligent Virtual Agent With a Mixed-Cultural Background. In *2023 11th International Conference on Affective Computing and Intelligent Interaction (ACII)*, 1–8. IEEE. https://doi.org/10.1109/ACII59096.2023.10388206

Oxford University Press. (2025a). *Artificial.* In Oxford English Dictionary (Online ed.). Retrieved February 5, 2025, from https://www.oed.com

Oxford University Press. (2025b). *Intelligence.* In Oxford English Dictionary (Online ed.). Retrieved February 5, 2025, from https://www.oed.com

Paiva, A., Leite, I., Boukricha, H., & Wachsmuth, I. (2017). Empathy in virtual agents and robots: A survey. *ACM Transactions on Interactive Intelligent Systems (TiiS), 7*(3), 1–40. https://doi.org/10.1145/2912150

Panch, T., Mattie, H., & Atun, R. (2019). Artificial intelligence and algorithmic bias: implications for health systems. *Journal of global health, 9*(2). https://doi.org/10.7189/jogh.09.020318

Parish, M., & Eagle, M. N. (2003). Attachment to the therapist. *Psychoanalytic Psychology, 20*(2), 271. https://doi.org/10.1037/0736-9735.20.2.271

Parmar, D., Olafsson, S., Utami, D., Murali, P., & Bickmore, T. (2022). Designing empathic virtual agents: manipulating animation, voice, rendering, and empathy to create persuasive agents. *Autonomous agents and multi-agent systems, 36*(1), 17. https://doi.org/10.1007/s10458-021-09539-1

Parsons, T. D., & Rizzo, A. A. (2008). Affective outcomes of virtual reality exposure therapy for anxiety and specific phobias: A meta-analysis. *Journal of behavior therapy and experimental psychiatry, 39*(3), 250–261. https://doi.org/10.1016/j.jbtep.2007.07.007

Pickard, M. D., Roster, C. A., & Chen, Y. (2016). Revealing sensitive information in personal interviews: Is self-disclosure easier with humans or avatars and under what conditions?. *Computers in Human Behavior, 65*, 23–30. https://doi.org/10.1016/j.chb.2016.08.004

Polanczyk, G. V., Salum, G. A., Sugaya, L. S., Caye, A., & Rohde, L. A. (2015). Annual research review: A meta-analysis of the worldwide prevalence of mental disorders in children and adolescents. Journal of child psychology and psychiatry, 56(3), 345–365. https://doi.org/10.1111/jcpp.12381

Powers, M. B., & Emmelkamp, P. M. (2008). Virtual reality exposure therapy for anxiety disorders: A meta-analysis. *Journal of anxiety disorders, 22*(3), 561–569. https://doi.org/10.1016/j.janxdis.2007.04.006

Prolific. (2024). *Audience Checker Feature.* https://app.prolific.com/audience-checker

Qi, Y. (2024). Pilot Quasi-Experimental Research on the Effectiveness of the Woebot AI Chatbot for Reducing Mild Depression Symptoms among Athletes. *International Journal of Human–Computer Interaction, 41*(1), 452–459. https://doi.org/10.1080/10447318.2023.2301256

Rankin, C. H., Abrams, T., Barry, R. J., Bhatnagar, S., Clayton, D. F., Colombo, J., ... & Thompson, R. F. (2009). Habituation revisited: an updated and revised description of the behavioral characteristics of habituation. *Neurobiology of learning and memory, 92*(2), 135–138. https://doi.org/10.1016/j.nlm.2008.09.012

Raparthi, M., Dodda, S. B., Reddy, S. R. B., Thunki, P., Maruthi, S., & Ravichandran, P. (2021). Advancements in Natural Language Processing-A Comprehensive Review of AI Techniques. *Journal of Bioinformatics and Artificial Intelligence, 1*(1), 1–10.

Read, J., Haslam, N., Sayce, L., & Davies, E. (2006). Prejudice and schizophrenia: a review of the 'mental illness is an illness like any other' approach. *Acta Psychiatrica Scandinavica, 114*(5), 303–318. https://doi.org/10.1111/j.1600-0447.2006.00824.x

Reeves, B., & Nass, C. (1996). The media equation: How people treat computers, television, and new media like real people. *Cambridge, UK, 10*(10), 19–36.

Reinecke, J., Braun, H., Jacob, R., & Mehmet, Y. (2008). Akzeptanz der elektronischen Patientenakte—Erste Ergebnisse der Nutzerbefragungen. *Telemedizinführer Deutschland, 9.* https://pub.uni-bielefeld.de/record/1863396

Rimer, E., Husby, L. V., & Solem, S. (2021). Virtual reality exposure therapy for fear of heights: clinicians' attitudes become more positive after trying VRET. *Frontiers in psychology, 12,* Article 671871. https://doi.org/10.3389/fpsyg.2021.671871

Rossi, A., & Lenzini, G. (2020). Transparency by design in data-informed research: A collection of information design patterns. *Computer Law & Security Review, 37,* Article 105402. https://doi.org/10.1016/j.clsr.2020.105402

Rothbaum, B. O., Anderson, P., Zimand, E., Hodges, L., Lang, D., & Wilson, J. (2006). Virtual reality exposure therapy and standard (in vivo) exposure therapy in the treatment of fear of flying. *Behavior therapy, 37*(1), 80–90. https://doi.org/10.1016/j.beth.2005.04.004

Roy, S., Klinger, E., Légeron, P., Lauer, F., Chemin, I., & Nugues, P. (2003). Definition of a VR-based protocol to treat social phobia. *Cyberpsychology & behavior, 6*(4), 411–420. https://doi.org/10.1089/109493103322278808

Russell, S. J., & Norvig, P. (2016). *Artificial intelligence: a modern approach.* Pearson.
Sachverständigenrat Zur Begutachtung Der Entwicklung Im Gesundheitswesen Und In Der Pflege. (2024). *Nachhaltiger Einsatz einer knappen Ressource—Gutachten 2024 Fachkräfte im Gesundheitswesen.* https://doi.org/10.4126/FRL01-006473488

Safikhani, S., Holly, M., Kainz, A., & Pirker, J. (2021, December). The influence of In- VR questionnaire design on the user experience. In *Proceedings of the 27th ACM Symposium on Virtual Reality Software and Technology,* 1–8. https://doi.org/10.1145/3489849.3489884

Samek, W., & Müller, K. R. (2019). Towards explainable artificial intelligence. In *Explainable AI: interpreting, explaining and visualizing deep learning* (pp. 5–22). Cham: Springer International Publishing.

Schneiderman, N., Ironson, G., & Siegel, S. D. (2005). Stress and health: psychological, behavioral, and biological determinants. *Annu. Rev. Clin. Psychol., 1*(1), 607–628. https://doi.org/10.1146/annurev.clinpsy.1.102803.144141

Schuetzler, R. M., Giboney, J. S., Grimes, G. M., & Nunamaker Jr, J. F. (2018). The influence of conversational agent embodiment and conversational relevance on socially desirable responding. *Decision Support Systems, 114*, 94–102. https://doi.org/10.1016/j.dss.2018.08.011

Shin, D. (2020). User perceptions of algorithmic decisions in the personalized AI system: Perceptual evaluation of fairness, accountability, transparency, and explainability. *Journal of Broadcasting & Electronic Media, 64*(4), 541–565. https://doi.org/10.1080/08838151.2020.1843357

Shneiderman, B. (2022). *Human-centered AI*. Oxford University Press.

Slater, M. (2009). Place illusion and plausibility can lead to realistic behaviour in immersive virtual environments. *Philosophical Transactions of the Royal Society B: Biological Sciences, 364*(1535), 3549–3557. https://doi.org/10.1098/rstb.2009.0138

Slater, M., Banakou, D., Beacco, A., Gallego, J., Macia-Varela, F., & Oliva, R. (2022). A separate reality: An update on place illusion and plausibility in virtual reality. *Frontiers in virtual reality, 3*, Article 914392. https://doi.org/10.3389/frvir.2022.914392

Sleep Review Magazine. (2023). *Wearable tech detects users' stress levels during sleep*. Sleep Review. https://sleepreviewmag.com/sleep-diagnostics/consumer-sleep-tracking/wearable-sleep-trackers/wearable-tech-detects-users-stress-levels-sleep/

Smink, A. R., Frowijn, S., Van Reijmersdal, E. A., Van Noort, G., & Neijens, P. C. (2019). Try online before you buy: How does shopping with augmented reality affect brand responses and personal data disclosure. *Electronic Commerce Research and Applications, 35*, Article 100854. https://doi.org/10.1016/j.elerap.2019.100854

Statista. (2023). *Insights Compass 2023: Unleashing Artificial Intelligence's true potential*. Statista. Retrieved from https://www.statista.com/study/138971/insights-compass-2023-unleashing-artificial-intelligences-true-potential/

Steel, J. L. (1991). Interpersonal correlates of trust and self-disclosure. *Psychological Reports, 68*(3_suppl), 1319–1320. https://doi.org/10.2466/pr0.1991.68.3c.1319

Steinman, S. A., Wootton, B., & Tolin, D. F. (2016). Exposure therapy for anxiety disorders. In *Encyclopedia of mental health*. Academic Press. https://doi.org/10.1016/B978-0-12-397045-9.00266-4

Strickland, J. (2007). How virtual reality works. *How Stuff Works, 29*.

Suso-Ribera, C., Fernández-Álvarez, J., García-Palacios, A., Hoffman, H. G., Bretón- López, J., Banos, R. M., ... & Botella, C. (2019). Virtual reality, augmented reality, and in vivo exposure therapy: a preliminary comparison of treatment efficacy in small animal phobia. *Cyberpsychology, Behavior, and Social Networking, 22*(1), 31–38. https://doi.org/10.1089/cyber.2017.0672

Sweller, J. (2011). Cognitive load theory. In *Psychology of learning and motivation* (Vol. 55, pp. 37–76). Academic Press. https://doi.org/10.1016/B978-0-12-387691-1.00002-8

Taddei, S., & Contena, B. (2013). Privacy, trust and control: Which relationships with online self-disclosure?. *Computers in human behavior, 29*(3), 821–826. https://doi.org/10.1016/j.chb.2012.11.022

Tamborini, R., Novotny, E., Prabhu, S., Hofer, M., Grall, C., Klebig, B., ... & Bente, G. (2018). The effect of behavioral synchrony with black or white virtual agents on outgroup trust. *Computers in Human Behavior, 83*, 176–183. https://doi.org/10.1016/j.chb.2018.01.037

Tavory, T. (2024). Regulating AI in mental health: ethics of care perspective. *JMIR Mental Health, 11*(1), e58493. https://doi.org/10.2196/58493

Unity Technologies. (2024). Unity—Manual: Reverb zones. https://docs.unity3d.com/Manual/class-AudioReverbZone.html

Van Schaik, D. J., Klijn, A. F., Van Hout, H. P., Van Marwijk, H. W., Beekman, A. T., De Haan, M., & Van Dyck, R. (2004). Patients' preferences in the treatment of depressive disorder in primary care. *General hospital psychiatry, 26*(3), 184–189. https://doi.org/10.1016/j.genhosppsych.2003.12.001

Vaswani, A., Shazeer, N., Parmar, N., Uszkoreit, J., Jones, L., Gomez, A. N., ... & Polosukhin, I. (2017). Attention is all you need. *Advances in neural information processing systems, 30*. https://doi.org/10.48550/arXiv.1706.03762

Wang, I., & Ruiz, J. (2021). Examining the use of nonverbal communication in virtual agents. *International Journal of Human–Computer Interaction, 37*(17), 1648–1673. https://doi.org/10.1080/10447318.2021.1898851

Watson, D., Clark, L. A., & Tellegen, A. (1988). Development and validation of brief measures of positive and negative affect: the PANAS scales. *Journal of personality and social psychology, 54*(6), Article 1063. https://psycnet.apa.org/doi/10.1037/0022-3514.54.6.1063

Weiner, M. F., & Shuman, D. W. (1984). What patients don't tell their therapists. *Integrative Psychiatry*. https://psycnet.apa.org/record/1984-26585-001

Wheeless, L. R., & Grotz, J. (1977). The measurement of trust and its relationship to self-disclosure. *Human Communication Research, 3*(3), 250–257. https://doi.org/10.1111/j.1468-2958.1977.tb00523.x

WHO. (2005). Mental health: Facing the challenges, building solutions. In *Report from the WHO European Ministerial Conference*. WHO. https://iris.who.int/handle/10665/326566

Wienrich, C., & Obremski, D. (2024). The impact of transparency and expert-framing on trust in conversational AI (Working Paper No. 4715193). SSRN. https://doi.org/10.2139/ssrn.4715193

Wolf, M. J., Miller, K., & Grodzinsky, F. S. (2017). Why we should have seen that coming: comments on Microsoft's tay "experiment", and wider implications. *Acm Sigcas Computers and Society, 47*(3), 54–64.

World Federation for Mental Health. (2024). *World Mental Health Day 2024: It is time to prioritize mental health in the workplace*. https://wmhdofficial.com/

World Health Organization. (2022). *Mental disorders*. World Health Organization. https://www.who.int/news-room/fact-sheets/detail/mental-disorders

World Health Organization. (2024). *Suicide*. https://www.who.int/news-room/fact-sheets/detail/suicide

Wu, C. J., Raghavendra, R., Gupta, U., Acun, B., Ardalani, N., Maeng, K., ... & Hazelwood, K. (2022). Sustainable ai: Environmental implications, challenges and opportunities. *Proceedings of Machine Learning and Systems, 4*, 795–813. https://doi.org/10.48550/arXiv.2111.00364

Yang, X., Li, Y., & Lyu, S. (2019). Exposing deep fakes using inconsistent head poses. In *ICASSP 2019–2019 IEEE International Conference on Acoustics, Speech and Signal Processing (ICASSP)* (pp. 8261–8265). IEEE. https://doi.org/10.1109/ICASSP.2019.8683164

MIX
Papier aus verantwortungsvollen Quellen
Paper from responsible sources
FSC® C105338
FSC
www.fsc.org

If you have any concerns about our products,
you can contact us on
ProductSafety@springernature.com

In case Publisher is established outside the EU,
the EU authorized representative is:
Springer Nature Customer Service Center GmbH
Europaplatz 3, 69115 Heidelberg, Germany

Printed by Libri Plureos GmbH
in Hamburg, Germany